Critical Guides to French Texts

62 Rousseau: Julie, ou La Nouvelle Héloïse

Critical Guides to French Texts

EDITED BY ROGER LITTLE, WOLFGANG VAN EMDEN, DAVID WILLIAMS

ROUSSEAU

Julie, ou La Nouvelle Héloïse

R.J. Howells

Lecturer in French
Birkbeck College, London

Grant & Cutler Ltd
1986

Library of Congress Cataloging-in-Publication Data

Howells, R.J.
  Rousseau, Julie, ou, La nouvelle Héloïse.

  (Critical guides to French texts; 62)
  Bibliography: p.
  1. Rousseau, Jean-Jacques, 1712-1778. Nouvelle Héloïse. 2. Philosophy in
literature. I. Title. II. Title: Julie, ou, La nouvelle Héloïse. III. Series.
PQ2039.H6 1986   843'.5   86-25658
ISBN 0-7293-0256-3

I.S.B.N. 84-599-1742-8
DEPÓSITO LEGAL: V. 2.252 - 1986

Printed in Spain by
Artes Gráficas Soler, S.A., Valencia
for
GRANT & CUTLER LTD
55-57, GREAT MARLBOROUGH STREET, LONDON W1V 2AY
and
27, SOUTH MAIN STREET, WOLFEBORO, NH 03894-2069, USA

Contents

References

Following common practice, I shall call Rousseau's novel by its sub-title, *La Nouvelle Héloïse*. All quotations are from the Garnier-Flammarion edition. My references give the Part and the letter as well as the page number (e.g. II, 13, p.160), in order to situate the reference within the structure of the work and to facilitate the use of any other edition. For other works by Rousseau I have used the Bibliothèque de la Pléiade edition of the *Œuvres complètes*, modernising the spelling. Italicised numbers in parentheses refer to the numbered items in the Select Bibliography at the end of this volume.

Introduction

For modern readers, *La Nouvelle Héloïse* may not be an easy book. It seems very long, although not much happens. There are many 'digressions'. The characters appear to live at an excessively high emotional pitch, and express themselves in an overwrought style. In the later eighteenth century however this book was a runaway bestseller. Why was it such a success? Partly because it was published by a man already known for his eloquent denunciation of the values of contemporary society. The sophisticated were amused and even fascinated to read more. But the novel also aroused a popular response, in the form of letters to its author from readers who found that it gave public voice for the first time to their own dreams and ideals. Both these groups responded to its tone, its celebration of the natural and its double cult of passion and virtue. Today we can see that these are the marks of a particular period, which literary historians used to call Pre-Romantic. From the limitations of our own period, we have to learn to accept this different discourse and read within its conventions. And if we are at all familiar with European cultural tradition we shall recognise that this novel is very much part of that tradition, because it deals with passion and society, love and death.

La Nouvelle Héloïse is concerned with the desire for the absolute, and the frustrations of that desire. We may find the book difficult because it is immensely ambitious, and immensely rich. Its characters seek, and the novel tries to define, the conditions of total happiness. Having failed to find it in the old order of individualism, the lovers look for it in the new order of the collectivity. Exploring this relationship, the novel also explores that between nature and society, between past and present, between memory and sense-data, between free-will and determinism, between the spiritual and the material. But this is still a narrative fiction. These oppositions are lived by the characters and emerge from the story, or, rather, from their letters, the immediate and subjective form of narration that Rousseau uses. They write to each other, a closed group following the same adventure. Their divisions are shared, and explored within a common framework. The novel works dialectically, through opposition and transcendence, but its meaning remains ambiguous. This is a poetic novel, working on several levels. Rousseau orders his mass of material by repetition and rhythm, and draws upon the expressive resources of language so as to produce a kind of novel that was quite new. The passionate tone of the writing also reflects his own emotional involvement. This is less an imitation of reality than an alternative world. Rousseau is trying to create his ideal through writing.

His novel was born from his own sense of a lack in his life. This he tells us in Book IX of the *Confessions*, which gives a fascinating account of its genesis. I have preferred in the space available to concentrate on the literary product, but it might be useful to place his novel in relation to his life as a writer. Published in 1761, it is his only fully-developed prose fiction. In effect it stands between his major philosophical and his personal writings. Chronologically it follows the *Discours sur l'inégalité*, and dates from about the same time as *Du contrat social* and *Emile*. After the official condemnation of these last two works in 1762 and his flight from France, Rousseau turned increasingly to writing in defence of himself. His novel brings together his philosophical concerns, while heralding the intimate works to come. In a sense it offers more than both. Through the fictional and poetic form, we have a richer if less rigorous exploration of his thought than any treatise, and a more powerful expression of his personal myths than is possible in directly autobiographical writing.

It may also be helpful to give a summary of the story. Any summary inevitably involves selection and interpretation. In this case it also involves ignoring for the present the fact that Rousseau's chosen medium of narration is the letter. I offer however the following narrative account.

La Nouvelle Héloïse is an epistolary novel, in six Parts:

I. The tutor of Julie d'Etange, only daughter of a minor Swiss noble family, declares his love to her by letter. She replies. Committed to chastity, and knowing that Julie's father would not even consider her marriage to a commoner, the couple struggle to keep their love pure. But circumstance and desire lead to their sexual union. To allay her father's suspicions and protect her, the tutor is persuaded by her cousin Claire and his friend Lord Edouard to leave.

II. The tutor recovers from his initial despair and suspicion of his friends. For the sake of her parents, Julie refuses Lord Edouard's offer to take them to England under his protection. The tutor's long reports of his life in Paris are suddenly interrupted by the news from Julie that his letters have been discovered by her mother.

III. In a rapid series of exchanges we hear of the mother's illness and death, Julie's increased sense of guilt, her father's insistence that she renounce the tutor, her own illness and the tutor's secret visit, and her marriage to her father's choice the Baron de Wolmar. She explains at length her new understanding that this marriage is the best thing for all of them. Then she closes their correspondence. Dissuaded from suicide, her former lover takes service on a global expedition from England.

IV. Six years on, Claire is a widow with a daughter, Julie and Wolmar have two young sons. Suddenly they learn that Saint-Preux (the former tutor) is alive and has returned. All three invite him to Clarens, where Wolmar is to 'cure' him of his former love. Long accounts of the utopian domestic order at Clarens are linked with details of the cure. The climactic crisis of virtue for the former lovers is a 'promenade sur le lac'.

V. Further letters on Clarens, into which Saint-Preux now considers himself fully integrated. Claire joins the group, then Edouard with whom after one winter Saint-Preux leaves for Rome. There he is to prove his cure and repay friendship by aiding Edouard in his own crisis of passion. All are concerned over an ominous dream. Julie urges Claire to marry Saint-Preux.

VI. Claire refuses marriage, as does Edouard with the aid of Saint-Preux in Rome. He and Edouard are to live per-

manently at Clarens. But before they return Julie, having saved
her younger son from drowning, falls mortally ill. Saint-Preux
receives from Wolmar a long account of her last days, enclosed
with a letter from Julie saying that she realises as she dies that
she still loves him.

'Les Amours de milord Edouard Bomston' included as an
appendix in many modern editions, was written at the same time
as the letter-novel but not published then. Except in my
Bibliography (*20*), I am leaving it aside.

1. Love

Like most novels, *Julie, ou La Nouvelle Héloïse* is a love story. (We use the same word for both: romance.) It fits the romance tradition of a passionate sentimental attachment between a young and attractive heterosexual couple. She is younger than he. She is blonde, another ideal stereotype. Most often, then as now, this love faces obstacles which it eventually overcomes, and the young couple are then free to marry. Here however the couple, although they have been lovers, do not marry. Julie weds someone else. But the story does not end there. It goes on to deal with the domestic life of the husband and wife, who strangely invite the former lover to share it with them. He, and she, strive to put the past behind them.

The subject then is not only love but virtue. Rousseau's inter-textual subtitle invokes an earlier collection of letters around passion and renunciation. The twelfth-century Héloïse was violently separated from her tutor-lover Abelard. The letters that they wrote in later life as virtuous ecclesiastics, recalling the desires of their youth, had been much copied and adapted since the late seventeenth century as a portrait of the passions. Rousseau moves the emphasis back to the relation between carnal and spiritual love, and thus places himself in perhaps the greatest tradition of our culture. Behind the twelfth century stand Platonism and Christianity; with it begins the ethos of courtly love; from it stems the literature of idealised sexual passion that runs from Dante and Petrarch to the Northern Renaissance, through the romances to the romantics. In our own time a degenerate version of the topos is still the theme of our paperbacks and pop songs: 'You take me to Heaven'.

The Platonic tradition taught that everything on earth is a more or less imperfect copy of the pure forms or Ideas that exist in a higher world. We should work our way up to the light of those forms of knowledge — the good, the beautiful, the true —

through their shadowy approximations below. 'Platonic' love leads us from the sexual to the philosophical. But must we therefore quit the first? Christianity sees a similar problem. The New Testament tends to oppose spirit to flesh. Both traditions appear in the culture of mediaeval chivalry, which modifies the opposition by having the knight serve both God and his lady. With Dante's Beatrice and Petrarch's Laura, the lady shows the lover the way to the higher life. In these male fictions sexual love is sublimated and the woman angelised. The poetry of courtly love, Renaissance verse narratives, the pastoral, and the prose romances, are increasingly secular versions of the same tradition. In the period before Rousseau it lives through the genius of Racine, then Prévost, who give it back a Christian dimension in a new thematic of guilt and innocence. *La Nouvelle Héloïse* is the next renewal of the cult of sexual love — privilege and peril — and its problematical relation with earthly order and with the ideal.

In Rousseau's text the tradition is further secularised by the admixture of sentimental morality, but it is also given its fullest expression, its richest synthesis, since the Renaissance. First the neo-Platonic dimension. For Julie's tutor, 'le bon' and 'le beau' are one. We must seek out 'les exemples du très bon et du très beau'. 'L'âme s'élève, le cœur s'enflamme à la contemplation de ces divins modèles' (I, 12, p.30). The body is a portrait of the soul, which in turn bears the image of the Idea. 'Si j'adore les charmes de ta personne, n'est-ce pas surtout pour l'empreinte de cette âme sans tâche qui l'anime, et dont tous tes traits portent la divine enseigne' (I, 5, p.17). Julie seems to have felt 'la soif d'aimer' before encountering its particular and human object (I, 13, p.32). All lovers are indeed Platonists in their fervour for their ideal (II, 11); philosophy is a higher love. The pedagogic relationship is thus uniquely appropriate, but here it works both ways, for the tutor-lover and the pupil-mistress direct each other (I, 12). The lovers aspire to a Platonic identity — 'l'union des âmes' — which is ultimately not only a knowledge of but a return to the Divine whole.

In the courtly tradition too love leads to the ideal, figured by the woman. The tutor tells Julie 'Il semble que des passions humaines soient au-dessous d'une âme si sublime, et comme vous avez la beauté des anges, vous en avez la pureté' (I, 10, p.25). Lord Edouard explains to him later: 'Savez-vous ce qui vous a fait aimer toujours la vertu? Elle a pris à vos yeux la figure de cette femme adorable qui la représente si bien' (V, 1, p.396). Love bestows moral qualities: 'L'amour véritable est un feu dévorant qui porte son ardeur dans les autres sentiments, et les anime d'une vigueur nouvelle. C'est pour cela qu'on a dit que l'amour faisait des héros' (I, 12, pp.31-32). Like a mediaeval knight, Julie's lover suffers in order to merit his lady. He undergoes repeated 'épreuves' (I, 15, p.35). This chivalric light helps us see the significance of the name 'Saint-Preux', bestowed by Julie's cousin upon the young man (IV, 5, p.311). He is, or charmingly tries to be, valiant for virtue. His usual appelation is 'ami' (less often, 'amant'). We should give this its full Platonic weight: friend and lover of the ideal.

As in the romances, love is 'dès le premier jour', instant and overwhelming, fated and undying (I, 4). Such love is given only to a few privileged souls, a spiritual — and one might now add 'sentimental' — aristocracy. Julie and Saint-Preux, despite their harping on morality, make an almost aesthetic distinction between themselves and what they call the 'vulgaire'. Such self-regard has Cornelian echoes ('ce cœur qui vous aime n'est pas indigne du vôtre'). The experience of love is conveyed in two languages and several different codes. The Italian verses of Petrarch, Tasso, Marini and the contemporary Metastasio are incanted. Occasionally we meet the vocabulary of Christian mysticism (the 'torrent de délices qui vient inonder mon cœur' of I, 5). The threnodies on separation owe something to Racine. In the Petrarchan and *précieux* tradition, hyperbole and conceits are needed to convey the intensity and the paradoxes of love, which is a life-giving flame. But the 'feu dévorant' also destroys. It is life but also death: 'la source du poison qui me nourrit et me tue' (I, 1, p.10). To the tradition of love as the vital principle is added that of love as mortal.

In Rousseau's text love is constantly linked with death. Death offers Platonic identity, a return to the whole. It 'fixes' love, freeing one from the pain, the struggles, the inevitable instability of a passion subject to flesh and time. It is figured in the 'langueur' of Rousseau's lovers, and it is close to both their sexual encounters: at the first Julie is ill, at the second she stresses that they may be killed (I, 27ff., and I, 53ff.). It is the consummation of love: 'O mourons! ma douce amie...' It is the alternative to love: 'il faut enfin que j'expire à tes pieds ... ou dans tes bras'. Purer and surer, perhaps it is preferable. This shades into the opposite view of carnal love itself as death. The Platonic deprecation of the senses may point this way, as may the male medico-mystical notion of expending one's vital fluid, and most explicitly the Christian tradition. Julie calls her revelation of her love to the tutor 'une mort', and later, 'une passion plus terrible que la fièvre et le transport m'entraîne à ma perte'. This physical and moral disorder reflects spiritual death. Love is 'un mal': both hurt and evil. These Christian resonances of shame and guilt are drawn in Julie's first letter particularly from *Phèdre*. To them is added a new bourgeois cult of physical chastity, and of the family. Sexual love is forbidden — we have not left Racine, though we have joined modern psychological criticism — by the paternal interdiction.

Passion is opposed by society. This classic pattern is also explored in new ways. Rousseau's language is traditional and poetic. But his situation is prosaic. His setting is firmly located, contemporary, provincial and private — realist almost in the English way of Richardson. The obstacle to the marriage — clearly and ideologically marked off in the French manner — is the 'préjugé nobiliaire' of the Baron d'Etange. The social issue becomes philosophical when social injustice is contrasted with natural freedom. The lovers possess a 'première liberté' (I, 24, p.51). According to Lord Edouard, 'ce chaste nœud de la nature n'est soumis ni au pouvoir souverain ni à l'autorité paternelle' (II, 2, p.134). Natural law, asserts the tutor, vindicates their sexual union and obliges them to mutual fidelity (I, 31, p.62). Julie seems to agree in that she actively seeks — a scandal in social and in literary terms — to become pregnant. She conceives their child, in effect the mark of nature's approval. But then she miscarries, retrospectively the sign of Heavenly disapproval (I, 63, p.121; III, 18, p.253). Though her father's opposition is clearly wrong, she accepts his claims upon her. From the beginning she affirms that family bonds are natural, a view also accepted by the tutor (I, 20 and 21).

Sexual love is a source of both vice and virtue. This contradiction points to a graver objection. We seek stability, but love is unstable. Sexual passion is violent, 'les fureurs de l'amour'. One is carried up, then plunged down, as the letters of the lovers amply illustrate. It is disordered too in that it may find itself opposed to the legitimate claims of the family and society. Within the lover it may cause constant struggles, for it requires in him or her 'un combat éternel' between different desires, the lower and the higher self, the natural and the social. There are the perils of absence, change, time, 'l'oubli'. The ideal, furthermore, may be revealed to be an illusion. These problematical dimensions are sketched from the beginning, and they are set out by Julie in two long letters at the centre of the novel. She tells Saint-Preux of her marriage to Wolmar, at which 'une puissance inconnue sembla corriger tout à coup le désordre de mes affections' (III, 18, p.260). Marriage provides

> un attachement très tendre qui, pour n'être pas précisément de l'amour, n'en est pas moins doux et n'en est que plus durable. L'amour est accompagné d'une inquiétude continuelle de jalousie ou de privation ... Les amants ne voient jamais qu'eux ... Mais ... c'est son ardeur même qui le consume; il s'use avec la jeunesse ... tôt ou tard ... on se voit réciproquement tels qu'on est. On cherche avec étonnement l'objet qu'on aima ... (III, 20, pp.274-75).

Thus duty, prudence, wisdom, even happiness, require us to turn away from love.

The second half of the novel shows us Julie in her married state. Both she and Saint-Preux believe that they have put their love behind them. Her husband Wolmar tries to bring about scientifically what they seek morally: the obliteration in their minds of the past by the present. Julie meets her death as 'martyre de l'amour maternel' (VI, 11, p.546). But, having fought the good fight for virtue, she is almost glad to die. With the return of death in the novel comes the return of love, the final victory going to the passion for the absolute. Objectively, the Platonic idealisation, the moral renunciation, the cult of memory and the promise of a shared afterlife are one. They fix the object of love at a distance. Claire in effect had explained this to the lovers before Julie's marriage. 'Si l'amour est un désir qui s'irrite par les obstacles ..., il n'est pas bon qu'il soit content' (III, 7, p.235). And Julie comes eventually to realise it: 'malheur à qui n'a plus rien à désirer!' (VI, 8, p.528).

In *La Nouvelle Héloïse* the pursuit of the absolute in love is reflected in other ways too. I have tried to show that the account of sexual passion is an enormously ambitious synthesis of European tradition. The concern with the family unit, and the preoccupation with sentiment, are contributions from Rousseau's own period. Most specific to him — though owing something to the romance tradition — is the refusal to isolate heterosexual passion from other kinds of human love. One of these is *friendship*. Julie and Claire share 'la vive et tendre amitié qui nous unit presque dès le berceau' (I, 7, p.19). On friendship too is bestowed not only primary but Platonic status: Claire is 'unique et parfait modèle d'amitié' (II, 10, p.154). On the male side a similarly absolute bond unites Saint-Preux with Lord Edouard: 'il y a un certain unisson d'âmes qui s'aperçoit au premier instant, et nous fûmes familiers au bout de huit jours, mais pour toute la vie' (I, 45, p.80). Across the sexes Julie was and Claire will be 'amante' for Saint-Preux; but each throughout is his 'amie'. *Family* relationships are of equally great importance. Julie and Claire are first cousins. Julie tells her lover that she places her parents first in her affections. He in response weeps for the memory of his own father (I, 20 and 21). The family, a source of consolation even in the first half of the work, is the source of stability and harmony in the second.

Within these other relations too, the expression of affection can be very intense. Julie's embraces with her father (I, 63) have drawn the attention of Freudian critics. The embraces of friendship, between persons of the same age and sex, are likewise passionate. The tutor volunteers that he envies the affection between Julie and Claire: 'J'étais jaloux d'une amitié si tendre; je lui trouvais je ne sais quoi de plus intéressant que l'amour même'. His evocation of the women's mutual caresses is certainly erotic: 'quelle extase, de voir deux beautés si touchantes s'embrasser tendrement, le visage de l'une se pencher sur le sein de l'autre, leurs douces larmes se confondre ...' (I, 38, p.73). The male parallel is surely the climax to Part I of the novel, when Edouard carries off Saint-Preux. (The narrator is, again, of the other sex.) '"Viens, homme infortuné", lui a-t-il dit d'un ton pénétré, "viens verser tes douleurs dans ce cœur qui t'aime ...". A l'instant, il l'a porté d'un bras vigoureux dans la chaise, et ils sont partis en se tenant étroitement embrassés' (I, 65, p.128). It would I think be a mistake to read into these two scenes a repressed homosexuality. The second is a brief wild fantasy of rape, but Saint-Preux is hardly less the passive party with Julie too. The dream is rather of a passionate androgyny, which takes us back towards the Platonic tradition. Claire asks, in playful seriousness, 'L'âme a-t-elle un sexe?' (II, 5, p.144). There is a flight from sexuality — from which Edouard rescues the lover as the lover later in Rome will rescue him — towards stability and the ideal, but this is also a preference for sentiment and sensuality, with which Rousseau's whole text is suffused. And there is the dream of security, the embrace of a friend, a parent, a family.

Thus sexual, sentimental and familial relations are constantly confused. 'O ma charmante maîtresse! ô mon épouse, ma sœur, ma douce amie!' writes the lover to Julie (I, 55, p.99). She herself urges Edouard to become for Saint-Preux 'son consolateur, son protecteur, son ami, son père' (II, 6, p.146). The lover, imitating Julie, calls Claire 'cousine' as well as 'amie'. Claire in turn tells Julie, 'ton amant est mon ami, c'est-à-dire mon frère' (II, 5, p.143); later he becomes instead her 'child' (III, 7, p.234).

The sharing of such nomenclature reflects the sharing of loving relationships, and of feelings. Julie to her lover: 'Tu n'as pas un sentiment, mon bon ami, que mon cœur ne partage' (I, 39, p.75). Claire to Julie: 'tous nos sentiments nous sont communs' (I, 62, p.113). Thus their language too is shared. The

Second Preface notes and tries to explain this: 'Dans une société très intime, les styles se rapprochent ainsi que les caractères, et ... les amis confondant leurs âmes confondent aussi leurs manières de penser, de sentir et de dire' (p.585). *Feelings* are the matter and the language of the work. Feelings, not external events; good feelings, and 'pas une mauvaise action' throughout (p.573). Clearly this is Rousseau's 'pays de chimères', his own dream of harmony. Its radiant principle within the fiction is Julie. Her rule is institutionalised in the second half of the work, at Clarens, but it is recognised and affirmed in the first half too. Julie is the centre of love, adored by parents, servants, friends, the whole earthly city (II, 5, p.141). The lover contrasts this with his own disinherited state, 'errant, sans famille et presque sans patrie' (I, 21, p.41). The women — this is their role — (re)-constitute families into which the male wanderers may be integrated. The exiles Edouard and Wolmar are received, like Saint-Preux, into Julie's first family, then into her second.

2. 'Digressions' and Myths

The Novel has been described (by Henry James) as 'a loose, baggy monster'. One of the many capacities of narrative fiction has always been the discussion of general issues. In some Enlightenment French fiction the point could be put the other way. The story is a pretext for the debating of questions which are presented to the public more digestibly, and perhaps less riskily, in the context of a story. The low status of prose fiction at this time, and the didactic theory of art, also led writers of imaginative works in this direction.

Rousseau's novel, uniquely, contrives to wed the most intense individual experience with the most universal meaning. In my next chapter I shall look at an overall philosophical meaning which is organic to story and structure. Here my concern is what appear to be digressions. The novel contains a number of discursive set-pieces: letters given over to the examination of some general topic, usually of contemporary interest, varying from the duel to theology. Before considering these set-pieces individually, a few generalisations are possible. As Rousseau himself confirms elsewhere, the views expressed are usually close to his own. Where more than one opinion is given (as on suicide) this reflects his own ambivalence. His correspondents are never simply wrong (except where Saint-Preux plays the *naïf*). Even their most abstract positions are personal and authentic to a truth that they share, and, despite initial professions of modesty, they write with great conviction. Their views and their tone are characteristically absolute, and dismissive of opinions and persons outside the group. They sometimes claim, on Rousseau's behalf, that these views are not only original but the antithesis of conventional wisdom. (The assertion is valid on the issue of education: V, 3, p.438. It is invalid on the account of 'les Parisiennes': II, 21, p.199.) Rousseau skilfully varies his mode of presentation, which may be anything from the straightforward statement of the writer's opinion (I, 57) to the narrative of a lively discussion (I, 62). Some of these set-pieces have been justifiably criticised for their awkwardness in relation to the narrative. In terms of overall thematic structure, however, it is worth noting that the 'digressions' appear to have a logic. The early ones are mainly on issues concerning the individual (jealousy, honour). Then we expand into the social (the bad society of Paris in II, the good of Clarens in IV and V). In the last Parts we reach a third level, transcendental religion.

I shall now look at the 'digressions' individually. The long series on *Paris* (II, 14-27) seem to me the least satisfactory. The approach and tone are uncertain, so that the letters succeed neither as a dispassionate description, nor as satire, nor as a philosophical analysis of causes. The use of Julie to criticise the tutor's adverse account perhaps reveals the same uncertainty on another level. The ambivalence is certainly that of Rousseau himself, the Swiss who had come to Paris as a young man to seek his fortune (and who would choose to live his last years there). While condemning the frivolity and decadence of the French upper classes, he admired their social virtues and was attracted by their elegance.

Those on Clarens I shall consider separately in chapter 4, except for that on *education* (V, 3). The latter might be linked with I, 12, which sets out the tutor's study programme for Julie. In both letters education is inseparable from moral dispositions, and in both the emphasis is on quality not quantity. Beyond this there are marked differences. Julie at 18 is already revealed as a 'belle âme'. She need only build upon her innate excellence, through a morality of imitation. (The dishonesty of the final paragraph, on 'livres d'amour', reflects ambiguities in Rousseau's position which I look at in chapter 6.) V, 3 concerns itself with general questions of education in its fullest sense. Here it appears that innate excellence may be the exception. Indeed even the natural goodness which is an article of faith in *Emile* seems to be in doubt. Wolmar appears to take this position, but then retreats (pp.426-27). (Rousseau also confuses matters by requiring him to contradict his own 'matérialisme du sage' (see my chapter 4), in order to rebut the more extreme environmental determinism of Helvétius.) The general question is simply abandoned in Julie's conclusion: 'Heureux les enfants bien-nés!' Some children are born with fortunate dispositions. She trusts that these include her own. She wants above all to see her children happy (p.429).

The essential principles of education are then set out much as they will be in *Emile*. They follow nature. Education for young children should be 'negative', in the sense of protecting them from all adverse or corrupting influences, and of allowing them to develop at their own pace. It should be 'l'éducation des choses', which avoids provoking the confusion and resentment that is aroused in children by reasoned human interdictions, while developing their physical skills and their awareness of the natural environment. It must teach them 'la loi de la nécessité', which makes them recognise their limitations, and learn as a function of their own needs. My second clause in each case summarises the 'modern' side of Rousseau's thinking, the first indicates his moral anxiety and his underlying pessimism. As in *Emile*, the educator must be ever-vigilant, the environment systematically controlled and the pupil manipulated. For the rural population at large, the 'negative' intention of nature is more easily assisted. The peasants are still in their natural condition, and need only be kept there. They should not be educated because it will make them dissatisfied and corrupt: unhappy as individuals; pernicious as an element in society (see too IV, 10). For Julie's children there are perhaps two differences. First, an elaborate controlled environment has to be created to replace and reproduce the natural. Second, a further stage of education will follow to develop their reason, and to fit them for their role among the privileged in society (p.437). But for this we must go to the latter part of *Emile*. Significantly, Julie's children are boys too.

The subject of *religion* appears in a number of letters towards the end of the novel. III, 18, in relation to universal and social order; V, 3 and V, 5, on Wolmar's religious scepticism; VI, 6-8, in which Julie and Saint-Preux offer complementary views; and Julie's formal profession of faith in VI, 11. As education is tied into the story by Saint-Preux's role as tutor, religion is also linked to the domestic situation. It is fairly clear that Julie's death will convert Wolmar, the reluctant unbeliever. But convert him to what?

Much of what Rousseau argues through Julie and Saint-Preux is fairly standard deism. God is a principle of justice and order. We know of His existence by the harmony of the universe, and by an interior sense. The complexities of theology may be ignored. God does not ask us to believe what we cannot; truth is simple. The essence of Christianity is the moral law, which we must follow on earth. (Julie's profession, on pp.532-33, offers useful summaries of these points.) Christ and the Redemption have no place here, but the notions of sin and grace however are briefly admitted, by Julie (pp.511-12). By comparison with deism, Julie and Saint-Preux rather deprecate 'reason' and espouse immediate conviction (p.520). There is a mystical dimension in Julie. Of the Divinity she has a sensual apprehension that is both intimate ('elle nous a donné ce degré de sensibilité qui l'aperçoit et la touche', p.533) and pantheist ('mon âme ... est toute dans l'Etre immense qu'elle contemple', p.529). Indeed God is not just the usual dispenser of rewards and punishments in the afterlife, He is 'present' now as a witness to the hearts of Saint-Preux and of Julie (pp.449, 545), and as a consolation. These new dimensions will appear again in Rousseau, but not so much in the didactic formality of the 'Vicaire savoyard' (*Emile*, IV) as in the later personal writings.

Turning back now to Part I of the novel, we find a rather different kind of 'digression'. In these cases the narrative situation is more immediately present. The tutor is usually at the centre, and the letters are about him if not also by him. Rousseau identified himself with the tutor (as he tells us in Book 9 of the *Confessions*). In all these ways the early pieces are more intimate. Dramatised through the tutor they reveal two kinds of myth: certain private imperatives in their real author; and the world he wanted to create in his novel.

Several of these letters are on *personal honour*. I, 15-18, on accepting money gifts; I, 24-25, on accepting a salary; I, 56-61, on the duel. We might add I, 62, and III, 11, on birth versus merit. Conventional though the latter topics are, all undoubtedly relate to Rousseau's own life, reflecting the sensibility of the commoner seeking recognition in an aristocratic and wealthy milieu. The narrative in which they occur reveals several kinds of fantasy, one of which is to be an aristocrat oneself. Like other bourgeois writers of his time, Rousseau deplores the ethos of the duel but is attracted by it. Despite the humanitarian and logical arguments systematically set out by Julie, it is made clear that the tutor would have fought. She saves him by her disarming letter to the great duellist Edouard, who thereupon kneels to him and becomes his protector. The utter improbability of the whole episode points us to the mythical imperatives underlying it. The tutor establishes his independence of Julie and his recognition as an equal by Edouard. He nevertheless remains passive throughout while others act around him, in his ignorance and for his benefit. They are in effect his protectors; he is their equal and yet their child. This pattern occurs throughout the novel.

The tutor's refusal of a salary confirms this, and brings in another level. The refusal is again aristocratic, and again passive, but it signals more clearly the tutor's unique 'fidélité' to his trust and to himself (see too the latter part of the letter on jealousy: I, 35). Tutorship has a special status. The initial situation — the unpaid tutor in the noble female household — is itself most unlikely, and should be seen as the first sketch of the ideal small society (tutorship here is reciprocal). The hostility to money reflects Rousseau's horror of intermediaries which corrupt relationships. This appears not only in the lovers' pursuit of the immediate 'Platonic' communication of souls, but as an economic principle minimising the use of money at Clarens. The personal and collective themes are profoundly linked to the mythical. The tutor's refusal of a salary will not save the ideal from corruption, because Julie's father is resolved to expel him. Society must corrupt. Paradise will be lost. But he will not be responsible.

Another sketch for the ideal society is the account of the *Haut-Valais* (I, 23). Again money is deprecated, and there is no trade with the outside world. Life is simple, agricultural, patriarchal, familial. The goodness of this society is preserved by nature itself, through its geographical isolation. But it also requires voluntary repression, in that the Valaisans refrain from mining the gold underground (pp.46-47). And it does not satisfy the tutor, whose desires break bounds and surface most improperly. The object of his desire, Julie's perfect breast, is more subtly veiled. He wants not just the transparent wholesomeness of the Valais but the provoking elegance of superior creatures. Again this is an anticipation of Clarens, in which everything must be gathered. The tutor celebrates, in the Valais, 'un mélange étonnant de nature sauvage et de nature cultivée', '[un] accord inconnu', and added 'illusions' (p.44). He calls it 'un nouveau monde' (p.45).

The two letters on *Italian music* (I, 48 and 52) may seem quite irrelevant. In fact the first is not only one more expression of the ideal: it declares in effect the quality and the mood of Rousseau's new world, that of his novel itself. Letter 48 begins with an exclamation, because the new world is a sudden revelation. The old world of French music acted upon us only 'indirectement et légèrement'. But Italian has 'le pouvoir d'agiter les cœurs'. The first is unaccented and mannered. The second is expressive, through 'le lien puissant et secret des passions avec les sons': an organic and poetic quality that Rousseau undoubtedly seeks in his own use of language. It possesses 'l'accent oratoire et pathétique', an excellent definition of Rousseau's own style. It speaks from the heart of 'celui qui se fait entendre', straight to the heart of the listener — or should we not say the reader? The previous world had involved 'pénibles efforts', 'contrainte' and 'combat', but the one newly discovered voluptuously flows, for 'tous les concertants sembl[ent] animés du même esprit'. Rousseau appears nevertheless to deprecate harmony in favour of the single voice, but this contradiction too can be reconciled within his novel: 'de toutes les harmonies, il n'y en a point d'aussi agréable que le chant à l'unisson' (V, 7, p.461). Reading on a different level, let us note finally that this new world is placed under the patronage of Julie's brother, who is dead. Thus it is a world from the past (see the epigraph to the novel). It is the world of the tutor, who is both a substitute for Julie's brother and the writer of this letter;

thus in turn it is the world of the originating persona and writer Rousseau.

Lastly the letters on *suicide* (III, 21 and 22), which serve to introduce my next chapter. The tutor, favouring suicide, pleads the case from nature. 'Chercher son bien et fuir son mal en ce qui n'offense point autrui, c'est le droit de la nature.' But 'combattre et souffrir' is our fate in all society, and therefore the individual may do away with himself. Edouard in reply pleads the case for society, change and time. 'Change donc ..., corrige tes affections déréglées', 'plusieurs siècles de jeunesse [nous apprennent] qu'il n'y a rien de meilleur que la vertu.' Think of your 'devoirs', think of 'la société'. Adopt '[une] vie active et morale'. 'Attends et tu seras guéri.'

3. A Philosophical Novel

All Rousseau's major philosophical works tell and retell the one story: that of the movement from nature to society. The first is the *Discours sur l'inégalité*. There Part I presents man in the state of nature, a creature of instinct, independent, spontaneous and innocent. Part II traces change, and the development through social relations of human self-consciousness and moral freedom. But, because social relations are bad, this is also the development of corruption and alienation. That is the actual history of the race, which went terribly wrong. It is also the history of each individual — from infant to adult — which parallels that of the race. The three great works published in 1761-62 are all attempts to rewrite that history as it should be. *Du contrat social* proposes a rectified history of the race. It sets out the preconditions of a legitimate social order in which collective man would not be corrupt. *Emile* on the other hand accepts the reality of bad societies. It sets out the pattern of an education based on nature which would form and preserve a good individual. From these works it appears that social man is both a natural and an unnatural phenomenon. Society is both within nature and against nature. *La Nouvelle Héloïse* follows through its protagonists the same itinerary and struggles with the same problem.

The lovers Julie and Saint-Preux represent all humanity. They are unique among humankind, says Edouard, precisely because their characters reveal the universal model. 'C'est cela même qui vous distingue, qu'il est impossible de vous distinguer, et que les traits du modèle commun, dont quelqu'un manque toujours à chaque individu, brillent tous également dans les vôtres' (II, 3, p.137). This is the model of nature: 'ces deux belles âmes sortirent l'une pour l'autre des mains de la nature' (II, 2, p.134). They possess therefore 'leur première liberté' (I, 24, p.51). Primal too is their youth — childhood of the race — and authenticity. It is appropriately in the very first letter that the tutor affirms of them both, 'si jeunes encore, rien n'altère en nous les penchants de la nature' (I, 1, p.10). Julie likens their early condition to that of Eden: 'l'accord de l'amour et de l'innocence me semble être le paradis sur la terre'. Change, of any kind, can only be for the worse: 'la moindre altération à notre situation présente me paraît ne pouvoir être qu'un mal' (I, 9, p.24).

These two are beings according to nature, and their love has a natural legitimacy. In both respects this puts them in opposition to society, whose false values forbid their love. Yet they themselves live in society, morally conscious of their obligations. Julie has a family to whom her ties are still more 'natural' than those to her lover. The inevitable result is conflict within the self. It is the crueller in that each lover possesses to a unique degree the aspiration to virtue, yet also the 'faiblesse' (III, 18, p.252; IV, 14, p.383) which is natural to man. The conflicts are both static and progressive. Their love forbidden, they fall from sexual virtue despite their best efforts. They must put on for others a false appearance, 'être si différent de soi-même' (I, 33, p.65). They suffer doubly, from 'une conscience avilie' (I, 63, p.117) and from 'la dure espèce de combat ... que le devoir nous demande, ... une résistance à des peines sans relâche' (I, 25, p.52).

The novel reveals, in temporal sequence, progressively larger social rings around the lovers. In I, 1-5, they are in the primal state of isolation. Then we discover Claire, the families, culture (I, 12), a different society in the Valais, the troubles of others ... and ever more resolute social opposition. At the same time love seeks ever more hidden sanctuary: 'le mystère du bosquet', the chalet as 'asile aux amants', Julie's bedroom as 'sanctuaire' (I, 13-14, 36, 54). Part II takes the lover to Paris, the formal 'entrée dans le monde' (II, 14). Now he is at the centre of life in society, which is explicitly contrasted with the primal, the rural and the simple which connote nature. Is it possible to 'conserver dans Paris la simplicité des antiques mœurs helvétiques' (II, 26, p.212)? Alas no. In the corrupt society the natural man, despite his love of virtue, eventually falls (II, 26). The increasing crises of Part III parallel the paroxysms of all humanity plunging into conflictual society in the *Discours sur l'inégalité*. But in the later works Rousseau rewrites the story as it should be. 'Alors cet état primitif ne peut plus subsister, et le genre humain périrait s'il ne changeait sa manière d'être' (*Du contrat social*, I, 6). 'Nous naissons, pour ainsi dire, en deux fois' (*Emile*, IV, p.489). *La Nouvelle Héloïse* too finds the solution to apparently inevitable corruption. The lovers must abandon their doomed natural relationship: 'nous périssions si nous n'eussions péri' (III, 20, p.278). The radical renewal, the rebirth to society, is Julie's marriage. 'Je crus me sentir renaître; je crus recommencer une autre vie' (III, 18, p.261).

Julie's first great letter to Saint-Preux on her marriage itself retraces the itinerary. Their relationship has gone from 'ces temps de bonheur et d'innocence', through 'ces longs combats' to the criminal adultery they were contemplating. This appalling degeneration from nature is the history of all humanity: 'Combien de siècles ont pu produire ce changement étrange?' At the same time the moral contrast is experienced by the individual like an instant, waking nightmare. 'On s'égare un seul moment ...; aussitôt une pente inévitable nous entraîne et nous perd; on tombe dans le gouffre, et l'on se réveille épouvanté de se trouver couvert de crimes, avec un cœur né pour la vertu' (p.260). Man naturally loves virtue and seeks order. Spontaneity, feeling, love, can lift him to the highest moral plane, but they can also leave him weak. They are self-generated and unreliable. In my first chapter I showed how Julie realises that love is an insufficient foundation for marriage. Like the rest of the story, her words must now be reread in this full philosophical context. Natural dispositions are an insufficient basis for life in society.

The equivalence between marriage and the social order is explicit. Julie writes of 'la sainteté du mariage, ... ses chastes et sublimes devoirs si importants au bonheur, à l'ordre, à la paix, à la durée du genre humain' (p.260); 'on ne s'épouse point pour penser uniquement l'un à l'autre, mais pour remplir conjointement les devoirs de la vie civile' (pp.274-75). Marriage signifies the social contract. *Du contrat social* advances the notion of conforming to a general will which forces one to be free, and so does Julie. She prays to the Supreme Being, 'Rends toutes mes actions conformes à ma volonté constante, qui est la tienne', so as to 'me rend[re] à moi malgré moi-même' (pp.262-63). But Emile too addresses the same plea to his teacher: 'Je veux obéir à vos lois, je le veux toujours, c'est ma volonté constante ...; forcez-moi d'être mon propre maître en obéissant ... à ma raison'. At this point the narrator says 'il aura, pour ainsi dire, signé le contrat' (*Emile*, IV, pp.651-53). This is, in all three works, the 'heureuse révolution' which returns imperilled humanity to order. The morally-free creature must choose to conform to an external order which both negates and strengthens his natural penchants.

Only in *La Nouvelle Héloïse* is the 'heureuse révolution' treated at length through the experience of a participant.[1] Julie's rigorous account stands both inside and outside the event. Just what is going on? She reaches the church as 'une victime impure', corrupted by society, divided and desperate. But there she is suddenly overwhelmed. She senses the human collectivity and the Divinity, all witnessing her. Then, perhaps the essential statement, 'une puissance inconnue sembla corriger tout à coup le désordre de mes affections et les rétablir selon la loi du devoir et de la nature' (p.260). The resolution of this disorder she had long sought, by an 'heureux instinct' within herself (p.263), but had not known where to find it. That it has now been given to her is likewise 'heureux': both chance and Providence. But it is precisely because of the natural instinct that she can now recognise it and that she will passionately — despite herself — conform to it. The paradoxical relation of natural to social order is equally evident in the change that occurs. 'Dans ce bouleversement général on reprend quelquefois son caractère primitif' (p.268). The revolution complements the instinct, enabling her to re-become herself. It serves, as she says, to 'rétablir' a primitive order, but to re-establish it on a new and sound basis, by adding the law of reason and institution to that of affection.

---

[1] Rousseau's own revolutionary experience, the 'illumination de Vincennes', is recounted notably in the second of the *Lettres à Malesherbes*. The story of his life as innocence, degeneration, revelation and attempted returns to order may be read there or in the *Confessions*.

The old order depended on the individual and on passion, the new offers 'une règle plus sûre' which is collective and universal, reasoned, dutiful, stable and permanent. The new order is revealed to the fortunate participant by 'une puissance inconnue'. This power too is both part of oneself and an outside agent. It is objectified in *Du contrat social* as the Legislator, in *Emile* as the Teacher. The new harmony entered by Julie is then incorporated in her husband Wolmar. In him all contradictions are eliminated. Individual, social and universal are one. 'L'ordre qu'il a mis dans sa maison est l'image de celui qui règne au fond de son âme, et semble imiter dans un petit ménage l'ordre établi dans le gouvernement du monde' (p.274).

The social state is within nature. (As lovers Julie and the tutor had always pursued virtue and order; that which is according to Providence must be according to nature.) But it is also against nature. The opposition is marked not only thematically (sentiment versus reason; instability versus consistency) but through the story and the patterning of the characters. Julie marries, Saint-Preux does not. From the beginning Julie was part of a family and of a community, settled and social; he was 'errant, sans famille, et presque sans patrie'. She stays in the one place, going only from father to husband, while his journeys take him across land and sea alone. Throughout the relationship, she is the stronger and the more stable. Unlike man, woman is naturally sociable, according to Book V of *Emile*. Claire too marries, and Edouard too does not. But it is not just a question of gender. (In this novel all oppositions are also complementaries.) The general order is represented by the male Wolmar. He is the master of the community at Clarens, the setting of the second or socialising half of *La Nouvelle Héloïse*.

Saint-Preux, the natural man, is invited into that community. The invitation is extended jointly by Wolmar, Julie and Claire, who offer to 'cure' him; that is, to socialise him. This is the *philosophical* reason why he must come to Clarens. Thus, in a structure that resumes all those so far, the second half of the novel opposes and resumes the first half. For the two protagonists, the coherence of the good social order replaces the conflicts of the bad. The break for Julie was her marriage, for

Saint-Preux it is the six years of absence between the end of Part III and the beginning of Part IV. His too is a rebirth, for he will now begin *the same itinerary on a new basis*. He enters Julie's household once more. He rediscovers her, and Claire. He revisits in due course the estate, the orchard, the 'bosquet', Meillerie, Villeneuve, all the 'monuments des anciennes amours'. He relives, as does Julie, the dialectic of sexual love and virtue. Claire once more listens or reads, interprets, advises and shares.

The difference is that the itinerary is now determined not by the vagaries and violence of the bad society (the Baron d'Etange) but by the order of the good. Wolmar presides. The new set of 'épreuves' for Saint-Preux and for Julie is not random but scientifically planned by Wolmar. In the new dispensation their aspiration to virtue is not opposed but favoured by the conditions of this society. For us as for them the basic issue now runs as follows. Do natural qualities (I-III) provide a sufficient basis for the good society (IV-VI), or must we change? Claire presents the matter to Saint-Preux with perfect clarity, on Wolmar's behalf and then her own: 'Il prétend vous guérir, et dit que ni Julie, ni lui, ni vous, ni moi, ne pouvons être parfaitement heureux sans cela. Quoique j'attende beaucoup de sa sagesse, et plus de votre vertu, j'ignore quel sera le succès de cette entreprise' (IV, 5, pp.311-12). On his cure, or socialisation, depends the happiness of all of them (this is an affective and moral fact, but also the principle of the social contract which must be entered by all). Wolmar's reasoned cure will contribute much (that is, we must change). Saint-Preux's own passionate natural aspiration will contribute still more (we may remain ourselves). Yet, even in the good society, the outcome is not certain. This is the full 'épreuve', the theme, the drama and the suspense of Parts IV-VI, attempting to rewrite Parts I-III.

Wolmar is a scientific materialist. (On 'le matérialisme du sage', see *10* and the paragraph in my next chapter.) Benevolent and 'une âme sensible', he is very much one of the group, but he is guided by reason and almost devoid of passions. He can order the cure with the dispassionate consistency of an experiment. ('Epreuve' belongs to the vocabulary of science as well as of

chivalry.) His diagnosis of the situation is set out in IV, 12 and
14. Saint-Preux and Julie are sincerely virtuous, but they are still
in love with each other. This paradox is possible because each is
in love with a *past* version of the other. 'Otez-lui la mémoire, il
n'aura plus d'amour' (IV, 14, p.382). Each without realising it
believes in an essence, an unchanging continuity from past to
present. Wolmar's plan is not to deny the reality of the past;
indeed, he recognises its validity — that of love, aspiration to
virtue, nature — and its unique moral value (p.372). (The
ambivalence is in him too.) His plan is rather, he says carefully,
to show that the present is different (p.383). By gradual
conditioning Saint-Preux must come to recognise the reality of
changed time and situation. The break between the beloved past
and the here-and-now is that between the order of individual
passion and the order of civil marriage. 'A la place de sa
maîtresse je le force de voir toujours l'épouse d'un honnête
homme et la mère de mes enfants: j'efface un tableau par un
autre, et couvre le passé du présent' (pp.383-84). Natural man is
being forced to be free. On the level of narrative, Saint-Preux
returns to Clarens. On that of the materialist cure, he and Julie
must revisit all the monuments of their past in order to challenge
the idealised continuity of memory with the sense-data of the
present. On that of nature and society, they must enter that
changed order which aids and completes their own aspirations.

Complete socialisation in the good order should make one
free, good and happy. Saint-Preux will address his thanks to
Wolmar, the principle of order, in these terms: 'J'ai recouvré ma
raison par vos soins; redevenu libre et sain de cœur ...' He is
now able to put back into society what society has given him:
'J'étais mort aux vertus ainsi qu'au bonheur; je vous dois cette
vie morale à laquelle je me sens renaître. O mon bienfaiteur! ô
mon père! En me donnant à vous tout entier, je ne puis vous
offrir, comme à Dieu même, que les dons que je tiens de vous'
(V, 8, p.463). It appears that the cure has succeeded.

In an important sense it has. Julie too believes herself cured,
and claims to be totally happy. Saint-Preux too now has a place
in the social order. Yet, as I show at the end of my next chapter,
there are flaws in Clarens and a surviving lovesickness in the

couple that resists total cure. The social order is unquestionably a good. The resistance of the couple is minimal and passive. It is nevertheless clear: in Saint-Preux's refusal to enter civil marriage with Claire; in Julie's spiritual dissatisfaction and her willingness to die which prepare her rediscovery of her love for Saint-Preux.

Finally in this chapter I want to look at two problems raised by the 'philosophical' reading. The first concerns the identification of the lovers' passion (and of familial feelings) with nature. In most fictions of this period this would be no more than a sentimental commonplace. Juxtaposed with the unique rigour of Rousseau's thought however it requires more attention. Neither of these affections was in the state of nature, where relations between beings are minimal and undiscriminating. However, in the *Discours sur l'inégalité* and especially in the *Essai sur l'origine des langues* Rousseau also entertains the notion of a Golden Age of cabins and shepherds, in which interpersonal relations were developed to the point where affections were selective and yet still spontaneous, self-conscious and yet innocent (complex and yet still simple?). That he moreover claims this temporary equilibrium to be 'durable' indicates the vanquishing of philosophical rigour by mythical desire. In *La Nouvelle Héloïse* the brief but consistently-sought 'accord de l'amour et de l'innocence [qui] semble être le paradis sur la terre' is in the lover's itinerary the equivalent early stage. This too allows us to say that passion is in nature — but in a sense which for me slackens the dialectic of nature and society fundamental to Rousseau's thought.

One might add that there is always too in Rousseau's thought a temporal ambiguity in the relation between nature and society. Society comes after nature and is sometimes treated as having abolished nature (as in the *Discours sur l'inégalité*, and perhaps in *Du contrat social*). But nature is no less a permanent principle, still present in the social state and in social man (as in *Emile*). The relation is both diachronic and synchronic. Thus in Rousseau's novel the good — love, family affection, friendship — though always antecedent to the bad can still exist contemporaneously with the bad society. And such affective dispositions may be hailed as natural even though by Rousseau's own account they are engendered by the social development of mankind. We can even find him ignoring entirely the theory of a state of nature, simply treating certain individual dispositions as natural. Attributing them to Platonic 'modèles', as Rousseau's novel sometimes does, has this implication. But again this seems to lack rigour. It is his anthropological and historical account of human development which provides both Rousseau's originality and the structure of his thought. From isolated lover, through degeneration resultant upon social contradictions, to rebirth to virtue in the right civil order, *La Nouvelle Héloïse* is an allegory of that development.

This leads to a second and more classic problem in the interpretation of this novel. It concerns Clarens and the society of *Du contrat social*. To what extent does Clarens meet Rousseau's philosophical definition of the right social order? I have indicated various senses in which it does. Julie and then Saint-Preux are reborn into the universal order or 'volonté générale' of which Wolmar is the embodiment. Marriage represents the contract, connoting the civil life. Clarens is a place of activity, where one leads 'une vie laborieuse' (IV, 11, p.352). The organisation of life on the estate seems to be that which is appropriate to the collective social order of Geneva (IV, 10, p.342, Rousseau's note). More generally, its ends are pursued through carefully graded rewards and punishments, through emulation and example, all under the public eye (IV, 10). This is part of the systematic education or conditioning that is necessary in the good society, to free its members from contradiction by orientating them entirely towards the collective good (see *Du contrat social*, II, 7, and III, 2). Saint-Preux's social conditioning is Wolmar's parallel project for the individual (similar to that in *Emile*, Books IV and V). He too must cease to be a child and become a man (V, 1). He will join in the collective labour of the group (V, 7). However, Clarens is not a contractual society, not a 'république' (IV, 10, p.339). It is based on private property, the power of the few and the servitude of the many. The latter are happy and morally free in that they gladly conform to the good order around them, but they have not chosen it, and in that sense are not free. Neither is deliberate political will the basis of this society for the few — rather it is a happy affinity. Saint-Preux may come and go as he wishes. He is a charmingly inefficient worker. These are kinds of freedom not given to the citizen. 'Dépendance' between persons, elsewhere the root of corruption, is here the norm. Clarens is the good order, but it approximates less to a model of collective political society, more to an intimate ideal.

4. The Conditions of Happiness

As a cultural preoccupation, the search for present happiness is perhaps one of the inventions of the eighteenth century. The privileged classes seem less concerned with salvation, or glory. Their weakening religious and royalist convictions turn towards the new notion of 'bienfaisance', the cult of feeling, humanitarianism, solidarity. Increased social stability and material comforts probably contribute to a belief that one may seek positive and consistent satisfaction from this life. Nature and human nature are 'rehabilitated', seen as sources of good rather than evil. Now the old art of pleasure becomes, through physiological assumptions and a systematic approach, a new science. The 'théorie des sentiments agréables', as the title of one work has it, provides the basis for a new ethics. Abstract schemes for collective happiness, or ideal societies, are common in eighteenth-century writing. But Rousseau's exploration of some of these questions in *La Nouvelle Héloïse* is uniquely rigorous, intimate and existential.

La Nouvelle Héloïse has been called 'le roman du bonheur'. The first half is given to the passionate pursuit of happiness by the two lovers. They cannot attain it, or rather maintain it. This is due notably to the contradictions of society, but those contradictions are experienced and lived by the couple: they are internalised. In these creatures of sensibility, everything — despite their abstract rhetoric — is visceral. Virtue is not just an idea but a need, existentially inseparable from happiness, and the assurance of stability is an emotional necessity. A satisfied conscience is part of one's well-being. All the imperatives must be realised, all that one loves must be united and possessed. Faced with the parental interdiction, Julie and the tutor are offered Edouard's estate. Could one ask for more than this 'asile à l'amour et à l'innocence', this avatar of Clarens? 'Venez y serrer, à la face du ciel et des hommes, le doux nœud qui vous unit. Venez honorer de l'exemple de vos vertus un pays où elles seront adorées, et des gens simples portés à les imiter' (II, 3, p.138). Julie refuses. She refuses because *she wants everything*. Her parents must also be happy, a need which stems for her not just from guilt, or duty, or even from goodness, but because she aspires to go beyond love to total well-being. To Edouard she must reply (II, 6) that all he offers is not enough. 'C'est beaucoup pour l'amour; est-ce assez pour la félicité?'

She at last finds the resolution of these tensions, at her wedding. The duties of marriage she describes as 'si importants au bonheur, à l'ordre, à la paix, à la durée'. The terms are interchangeable but happiness is invoked first. The lover's reply to her account poses the vital question directly: 'Julie, êtes-vous heureuse?', to which her second great letter responds. In her marriage she finds not love, but happiness (III, 20). The latter half of the novel follows the progressive constitution of the group at Clarens, and it attempts systematically to create and define the conditions of their happiness. The ambition is, as ever, total, happiness requiring both freedom and order, both immediacy and unbroken continuity. The individual and the group, interior desires and external circumstances, the sensual, the affective, the moral and the universal must be at one.

Let us glance first at the whole society at Clarens. Clarens is at one and the same time unique and exemplary. It depends on the coincidence of a thousand rare circumstances; yet it is how all humankind should be (V, 3, pp.442-43). Rousseau offers both the most exact definition of these many circumstances and an idealised picture of this society. These are the characteristics we associate with the philosophical and literary genre known as *utopia*. More strictly, one can call Clarens a utopia in that it depicts a collectivity living in optimum conditions, and because this is a closed society (*13*, p.15). Like most utopias, it appears regimented and authoritarian. It is also — most obviously for the workers, the children and Saint-Preux — highly yet covertly manipulative. The determinist approach, the constant and carefully hidden social control, Wolmar's psychiatric 'cure' of the deviant individual, all strike a remarkably and alarmingly modern note for us. In my previous chapter I indicated some of

the reasons why Rousseau considers such systematic mani-
pulation necessary. His social determinism, the view that men
are conditioned by their social relations, is one reason for his
fundamental historical importance as a thinker. Beyond this
positive consideration too is his basic historical pessimism, and
underlying that is his personal insecurity. But let us turn now to
the novel's primary focus, the imperatives of the small group of
privileged souls at the centre.

The primary pre-condition for the attempt at total happiness
is the character of all the members of this group. They are 'de
belles âmes', 'des gens bien nés', possessing still that original
authenticity that enables them — rather, impels them — to seek
and recognise happiness. Clarens offers the second pre-
condition which is the right moral order. Here their imperatives
are without necessary conflict or contradiction. For the particular account of the life at Clarens we have five letters, all long
set-pieces, which could be classified as follows: the organisation
of the workers (IV, 10); the secret garden or 'Elysée' (IV, 11);
the economy of the masters (V, 2); philosophy of education (V,
3); the grape-harvest (V, 7). To some extent the letter on
education stands apart and I have treated it earlier. The others
offer not just a sequence but a dialectic. The labouring subaltern
society of the first letter finds its antithesis in the contemplative
and exclusive 'Elysée' of the second. The third then brings
together the 'économie' of the estate and that of Julie's sensibility. Finally the vintaging is the apotheosis of the collectivity
actually at work (complemented however by the intimate stasis
of the admirable 'matinée à l'anglaise' of V, 3). The grape is
associated with pastoral joy and Christian communion. The
event also marks natural 'convenance' and moral reward, for
the workers are harvesting the fruits of nature and their own
labours. Wolmar in addition is harvesting the recompense for
having re-created both the little society and its newly-integrated
member Saint-Preux. (On the 'Vendanges' see too 6, pp.116-29.)

'L'ordre et la règle qui multiplient et perpétuent l'usage des
biens, peuvent seuls transformer le plaisir en bonheur' (IV, 10,
p.349). This remarkable formula, in which almost every term
will be developed, directs at Clarens what Rousseau will call

'l'art de jouir'. But what is the existential reality within our-selves, the human exigency, to which 'la jouissance' must respond? 'Julie a l'âme et le corps également sensibles. La même délicatesse règne dans ses sentiments et dans ses organes. Elle était faite pour connaître et goûter tous les plaisirs, et longtemps elle n'aima si chèrement la vertu même que comme la plus douce des voluptés. Aujourd'hui qu'elle sent en paix cette volupté suprême, elle ne se refuse aucune de celles qui peuvent s'associer avec celle-là' (V, 2, p.409). The principle of her being is not thought, not will, not virtue, but sensibility. Like love, of which it is perhaps the undifferentiating and primary form, sensibility is a great burden as well as a privilege. In the tutor, as in Julie, it opens one to the most intense experiences, and it unites all levels of human experience. 'Que c'est un fatal présent du ciel qu'une âme sensible!' exclaimed the tutor much earlier, reviewing the suffering it brought. The man of sensibility is a 'vil jouet de l'air et des saisons'. Because he knows the good, he finds himself in contradiction with existing society; because he knows the ideal, 'il cherchera la félicité suprême sans se souvenir qu'il est homme' (I, 26, pp.53-54). Clarens resolves the second of these contradictions, and it makes the most serious attempt upon the third. The first implies the eighteenth-century doctrine of *sensation(al)ism*. The great importance to Rousseau of this view of man's relation to his physical environment might be explained as follows.

Locke had stressed that our knowledge of the world is built up from sense experience. More radical theorists of Rousseau's own time tried to move from Lockean sensationism to full materialism, that is, they denied the existence of any immaterial soul or independent principle of mind, and tried to explain man uniquely in terms of organic matter and combinations of sense stimuli. Rousseau readily adopts what we could call Locke's developmental psychology (of which Book II of *Emile* is the most profound exploration). On the other hand, he reacts passionately against atheist materialism, though he is persuaded of the view that our affective and indeed our moral being is radically influenced by our environment. He planned a treatise exploring this relation and demonstrating how 'un régime

extérieur varié selon les circonstances pouvait mettre ou main-
tenir l'âme dans l'état le plus favorable à la vertu'. The work was
to be entitled *La Morale sensitive, ou le matérialisme du sage*
(see *Confessions*, IX, p.409). It was never written. But in a way
everything that he did write reflects this view. All Rousseau
studies 'l'homme dans ses rapports' (see *La Nouvelle Héloïse*,
II, 16, p.172; V, 1, p.395). Each of his theoretical writings tries
not only to (re)situate but to *condition* man in the right relation
to the natural order. The *Rêveries du promeneur solitaire* show
us Rousseau's efforts to place himself under 'la loi de la
nécessité'. The state of 'rêverie' itself requires 'le concours des
objets environnants'. In *La Nouvelle Héloïse* the first account of
physical surroundings notes 'l'empire qu'ont sur nos passions les
plus vives ... une suite d'objets inanimés', concluding that 'un
heureux climat [peut] servir à la félicité de l'homme' (I, 23,
pp.44-45, on the Valais). The happy climate will eventually be
found. Julie's account of her conversion begins with her
physical surroundings, and Wolmar's cure of Saint-Preux is an
'éducation des choses', in that it would erase the past by the fact
of present sense-experience. But the opposed force of memory is
also aroused by sense experience, through the 'signe mémoratif'
(see my Chapter 5). In all these cases of course man is not a mere
tabula rasa to be written on by his environment: sentiment or
passion is already there. The privileging of its idealist form,
passion for the good, confirms that the Platonic-Christian hier-
archy is intact. To be the 'jouet de l'air et des saisons' is 'vil', for
the physical is considered inferior to the spiritual. But one
principle, sensibility, unites the levels, leaving us open to the
whole gamut and demanding the whole gamut. Sensation, sentiment, moral feeling and spiritual aspiration are to provide a
single 'volupté'. From Lockean epistemological theory, by way
of eighteenth-century rationalism, materialism and feeling, we
have come to the totalising ambition of the Romantics.

True to his own existential account of man in nature,
Rousseau's first rule of happiness is rudimentary and negative.
'Le premier pas vers le bonheur est de ne point souffrir' (V, 2,
p.401; see too III, 21, p.279). This is also, implicitly at least, a
form of that 'amour de soi' which is natural and legitimate in

man. Of Julie we are told, 'le mal-être lui est extrêmement sensible et pour elle et pour les autres'. That is, she suffers if there is any kind of ill-being (a doubly 'physical' term) in or around her (assimilation of self and environment). 'Il lui fallait pour être heureuse vivre parmi des gens heureux.' Thus she does good for her own pleasure: 'elle jouit du bien qu'elle fait'. She draws from this a satisfaction that is almost materialist: 'en sortant de chez elle ses yeux ne sont frappés que d'objets agréables'. Yet it is also exquisitely refined: 'cette âme si peu sensible à l'amour-propre apprend à s'aimer dans ses bienfaits'. Here too we see the outline of two 'movements' fundamental to Rousseau's concept and vocabulary of happiness. Appropriation ('en possédant mieux ce qu'il a ... [l'homme] jouit ..., il en fait son bien, ... il se l'approprie': IV, 10, p.350) implies both 'épanouissement' and 'recueillement'. The soul goes out to the whole world and tries to concentrate it in the self. Thus, again, referring to Julie, 'le bonheur qu'elle goûte se multiplie et s'étend autour d'elle'. However, 'ce serait sortir des termes de la raison que de faire dépendre son bonheur de celui de tous les hommes' (V, 2, pp.401-03). Even in the order of Clarens, there are limits.

Julie, like the whole institution, has to cope with these limits. The problem, in effect, is to achieve the maximum of permanent 'jouissance' while avoiding 'dépendance'. (The suggestion of drug dependence, to the modern ear, is not entirely inappropriate.) The solutions are a little strange. To avoid dependence, Julie rations her pleasures. Indeed, 'l'art de jouir est pour elle celui des privations'. This discipline, we are told, preserves her moral freedom: she avoids being dominated either by her appetites or by contingent circumstances. It is moreover a form of voluptuousness, because it preserves desire for another day, indeed for one's whole lifetime. The latter argument one would like to accept as existentially authentic, but of course Rousseau himself reverses it elsewhere, rather more persuasively ('C'est une bien cruelle prudence de rendre [une] portion [de la vie] malheureuse pour assurer le bonheur du reste': V, 3, p.430.) More revelatory perhaps is a linked explanation. 'Cette âme simple se conserve ainsi son premier ressort; son goût ne s'use point; elle n'a jamais besoin de le ranimer par des excès, et je la vois souvent savourer avec délices un plaisir d'enfant' (V, 2, p.409). Rousseau is once more in pursuit of a state of equilibrium which is primal ('simple', 'premier', 'enfant'). Our present refinement gives us far more ('goût', 'délices'); but this means that only through an elaborate system can we even re-approach the original identity. Equally notable is the antithesis 'se conserver'/'user', a vocabulary temporal and materialist.

As Julie, so the institution. M. de Wolmar seeks 'l'abondance du seul nécessaire ... [qui] a sa mesure naturelle'. 'Les vrais besoins n'ont jamais d'excès', whereas false social needs enslave because 'l'opinion est illimitée' (p.416). At the start of their establishment at Clarens, the couple took stock of their wealth, and finding their patrimony sufficient, 'ils se sont donc appliqués à l'améliorer plutôt qu'à l'étendre' (p.399). Seek the natural; conserve; limit and intensify. Remarkably, the estate lives entirely on its own production, thus drawing its sustenance immediately from nature, and ensuring its self-sufficiency. The system is such that its economic and moral independence is built in 'par la nature des choses' (p.417) — always Rousseau's aim. Trade and especially money are to be avoided, because they are intermediaries between production and consumption, but also because 'aucun de ces échanges ne se fait sans perte' (p.414). The materialist vocabulary again suggests a finite resource threatened by time and usage. In effect, to conserve the patri-mony we must block all the holes. Rousseau's 'épargne' implies a male sexual fear of using up the vital substance (compare II, 15, p.167). It is also moralistic, prudential and bourgeois. Yet it incorporates his rigorous philosophy of nature. It insists on sim-plicity yet is tortuously elaborate in pursuit of extreme aesthetic refinement. It reveals his constant desire to go back to immediacy and forward to totality. The text is extraordinarily rich.

Clarens is to be the place not only of reconciliation but of complete 'harmonie' (likewise we meet the terms 'concert' and 'accord'). With such an ambition, it is not surprising that the systems to realise it can seem strained and unconvincing. The letter on the 'Elysée' enables one to deconstruct the ideal fiction in other ways. (On this garden see too *23*, p.113-18.) The 'Elysée' is presented as a substitute both for orchard and for the 'bosquets si charmants et si négligés' which were the domain of the lovers (pp.353, 364), and is thus a fit emblem of the whole of Clarens. Like the whole, it contrives to bring together culture and nature. The role of the former is curiously minimised and maximised at the same time: 'la nature a tout fait, mais sous ma direction, et il n'y a rien là que je n'aie ordonné' (p.354). The principle of economy, and the reliance on nature, are assured by the claim that this considerable undertaking cost nothing. (The illusion of natural effortlessness is achieved for the whole too, by suppressing — between Parts III and IV — the half-dozen years abuilding. Through the account by Saint-Preux we come upon the finished article.) The 'Elysée' offers both the ultimate and the immediate, the ideal and the domestic: 'Julie, le bout du monde est à votre porte!' (p.353). Like Clarens, it is closed from the outside yet apparently infinite from the inside because art has contrived to 'cacher les bords de l'île' (p.359). The processing and false labelling of the wine (V, 2, pp.417-18) involves the same domestic appropriation of the universal through pretence. The hidden control practised in the 'Elysée' is ubiquitous at Clarens. 'Partout un air de profusion couvre l'ordre qui le donne' (p.416). It is used not only on plants but on human beings: 'tout l'art du maître est de cacher cette gêne ...' (p.339). In every case an elaborate 'supplément' attempts to replace the original immediate and necessary order in nature, encompass the infinite sought by social man, and erase itself. (See too my discussion of desire, in chapter 5).

It won't do. The extraordinary attention given to the realisation of Clarens both masks and reveals the lack of total belief behind it. There are the particular tensions one perceives in Rousseau's account. But we are also told that Clarens is permanently threatened both in principle and in practice. In principle it fails to meet its own absolute standards. The workers' institution is based on relations contrary to man's nature. 'La servitude est si peu naturelle à l'homme, qu'elle ne saurait exister sans quelque mécontentement' notes Saint-Preux (IV, 10, p.345). The whole cannot escape the law of instability and degeneration. 'C'est en vain, dit M. de Wolmar, qu'on prétend donner aux choses humaines une solidité qui n'est pas dans leur nature' (V, 2, p.400). Measured by nature and by time, Clarens is found wanting. But, secondly, it also fails existentially to satisfy its principal occupants. How significant it is that even within this retreat there are further retreats. The 'Elysée', the 'gynécée' (IV, 10), the 'salle d'Apollon' (V, 2), are all further refuges, islands within the island, 'asiles' within the 'asile'. Significant too here is the classical choice of names, connoting an ideal past; in the case of the 'Elysée' also death and ideal future. Nature, time, the past, death ... We are back to love.

Julie and Saint-Preux are both strongly committed to Clarens. They wish to be, and believe that they are, part of the wider and active order of the present, but, again, anxiety betrays the sense of a gap between the aspiration and the experience. As before, their roles here are parallel yet complementary. Saint-Preux is the one who repeatedly backslides. Near the end of the 'Elysée' letter, he twice harks back to the guilty past. He is rebuked and rebukes himself, resolving not to let this happen again. But it does: above Meillerie, at the grape-harvest, at Villeneuve. His failures exhibit his childlike quality, and — thus — a certain fidelity to nature. Julie as always is stronger, her fidelity being to the social order of husband and children, and perhaps to her own dignity. She writes less. Nevertheless she admits that she had feared the arrival of Saint-Preux (IV, 7). Believing that her heart has really changed she lets slip a word of regret: 'Je m'en félicitai *tristement*...' (IV, 12, p.372, my emphasis). At Meillerie it is clear that not Wolmar's cure but her own virtue saved the present order from the past (IV, 17, p.392).

Once more the central paradox: society negates and builds on nature. In society Mme de Wolmar is happy and cured, yet she draws her capacity for happiness and her will to be cured from nature. Sometimes she attributes her cure to society (VI, 6, p.505), sometimes to nature and 'le véritable amour' (VI, 8, p.524). At Clarens she experiences and possesses total happiness. 'Tout l'univers est ici pour moi ...; je ne vois rien qui n'étende mon être, et rien qui le divise ...; je n'ai rien à désirer; sentir et jouir sont pour moi la même chose; je vis à la fois dans tout ce que j'aime, je me rassasie de bonheur et de vie' (p.525). Yet Claire observed that her whole life had been 'un combat continuel' (IV, 13, p.378). Her own final letter, revealing her suppressed love for Saint-Preux, tells us that Claire was right. Her penultimate letter announced a different dissatisfaction. While sincerely proclaiming her total happiness, she went on to contradict this. 'Mon ami, je suis trop heureuse; le bonheur m'ennuie'; 'mon âme avide cherche ailleurs de quoi la remplir' (pp.528-29). For her, even at Clarens, the project for earthly happiness falls short of the ideal. Or shall we say that Rousseau makes sure that it falls short? He strongly recommends Clarens, the possibility of a fully satisfying social order on earth. But he makes sure that the 'cure' fails for the lovers, in order to preserve for them — ultimately for himself — the margin of freedom and unsatisfied desire.

5. Memory, Distance, Desire

All Rousseau's writings are concerned with time. Time is perceived as entailing loss and degeneration. Part I of the *Discours sur l'inégalité*, the state of nature, is *pre*historic in the strictest sense. It is a permanent state, pre-temporal in that change, degeneration, history (Part II) have not yet begun. It is also atemporal. For us as a philosophical model it is as valid now as then; and for those who lived in it there was no sense of time because they lived 'immediately', aware only of the present. The 'negative education' of *Emile* is to hold back time and change, so that the child remains as long as possible in the natural harmony of childhood. Later books of *Du contrat social* are much occupied with how to maintain the legitimate political institution against corruption over time. Rousseau's chief personal writings, the *Confessions* and the *Rêveries*, are chronological or fragmentary attempts to recapture his own past. His novel presents all these concerns, but here they are given greater intensity. They are lived, over a dozen years, through the fiction; they are presented from the inside as affective experience through the characters' letters; and they are mythologised by style and structural repetition.

My previous chapters have already touched upon time. Happiness required *unbroken temporal continuity*. Julie urged her lover that no change whatsoever be admitted to their 'temps de bonheur et d'innocence'. Change occurs. But the mark of the ideal human state remains the *fixing* of time. 'Quelle volupté pure, continue, universelle!' exclaims the tutor of his state after making love with Julie. 'C'est de toutes les heures de ma vie celle qui m'est la plus chère, et la seule que j'aurais voulu prolonger éternellement' (II, 55, p.98). As the private ideal, so the public. The apotheosis of Clarens, the 'Vendanges' letter, is narrated in the present tense. Of such days Saint-Preux concludes, 'on ne serait pas fâché de recommencer le lendemain, le surlendemain, et toute sa vie' (V, 7, p.462). The erotic state however cannot last, and Clarens does not. In Book VI Julie projects another continuous future, that of the 'séjour éternel', but she realises as she dies that it must encompass the past, 'le premier sentiment qui m'a fait vivre'.

Change turns the present into the past, but the past is accessible through *memory*. Rousseau links the philosophical and moral themes of the work to memory of the early time. Because love is assimilated to the Platonic ideal, the Good remains available through memory. How can the lover resist the corruptions of Paris? 'Songe surtout à nos premières amours', Julie urges him: 'Tant que ces moments purs et délicieux reviendront à ta mémoire, il n'est pas possible que ... le charme du beau moral s'efface dans ton âme' (II, 11, p.159). Love itself is preserved through memory, as Claire explained to the lovers. 'Le temps ... semble se fixer en votre faveur par votre séparation; vous serez toujours l'un pour l'autre à la fleur des ans; vous vous verrez sans cesse tels que vous vous vîtes en vous quittant' (III, 7, p.235). According to Wolmar later, Saint-Preux's love is really memory: 'Ôtez-lui la mémoire, il n'aura plus d'amour'. The effacing of the image in the memory by the image of the present is the basis of the 'cure' at Clarens. Thus memory is at the centre of an irresolvable contradiction. Happiness consists in remembering the past, and in abandoning the past. This is dramatised as the second half of the novel, in which Saint-Preux revisits the 'monuments' of love — the 'bosquet', Meillerie, and so on — so that the past may be both relived and exorcised.

Each of these places functions as a *signe mémoratif*. Wolmar's materialist cure requires the subject to re-experience his past as concretely as possible, through external stimuli and associative memory. But this is only an application of a fact in the affective lives of Julie, Claire and especially Saint-Preux. Physical objects once associated for us with a certain experience or sentiment have the power to evoke it again. It is Julie, during the absence of the tutor, who first observes on this: 'Tous les objets que j'aperçois me portent quelque idée de ta présence pour m'avertir que je t'ai perdu'. The experience is bitter-sweet:

'plus ton souvenir me désole, plus j'aime à me le rappeler' (I, 25, pp.52-53). By its association with the past, the object both marks the absence and invokes the presence. Memory restores the past to the present as an image. In the very last letter of the novel Claire experiences the presence of Julie in this way. For Saint-Preux the portrait of Julie, or the first letter he receives from her after many years, has a similar effect (II, 22; VI, 7). The classic formulation is offered by Saint-Preux when he revisits his rocky eyrie above Meillerie. 'En les revoyant moi-même après si longtemps, j'éprouvai combien la présence des objets peut ranimer puissamment les sentiments violents dont on fut agité près d'eux.' For him the place is so filled with 'celle dont l'image l'habitait jadis avec moi' that when he leaves (with Julie de Wolmar) he feels that he is quitting Julie (d'Etange) (IV, 17, pp.389-90). Still more overwhelming is the effect when at Villeneuve he re-enters the same room he had occupied during his initial banishment. 'J'en fus si vivement frappé que je crus redevenir à l'instant tout ce que j'étais alors: dix années s'effacèrent de ma vie et tous mes malheurs furent oubliés. Hélas! cette erreur fut courte' (V, 9, p.465). The recovery of the past is sudden, intense, a source of joy and pain.

Thus Rousseau gives close attention to the phenomenon of memory, including involuntary memory and its mechanism. Occurrences of involuntary memory are thematic and affective high points in the second half of the novel. This was quite new. Rousseau anticipates here not only the Romantics but Proust. Returning to the Vaud, writes Saint-Preux, the combined effect of place and memory 'semblait me rendre à la fois la jouissance de ma vie entière' (IV, 6, p.313). But there are of course important differences. In Rousseau's novel both the signs and the sentiments they evoke are more culturally elevated than they will be in Proust, and less exactly defined. In Rousseau, as later in most of the Romantics, they belong to received 'poetic' discourse. The signs are well prepared. (The room at Villeneuve, undistinguished and unexpected, is a notable exception; but Rousseau reinforces the effect by a dream and by the repetition of the Besançon episode.) The signs provide the itinerary of the narrative, but — officially at least — this itinerary is morally improving rather than constituting its own *raison d'être*. This being a letter-novel, they cannot provide a structuring principle of narration that replaces chronology by a single re-organising consciousness. Emphasis here is less on the coincidence of two moments than on the reliving of a past sentiment. What Rousseau's writing conveys most marvellously is the meta-phorical expansion or contraction of time to express affective continuity or intensity ('une éternité', 'un moment'), and the cult of a plenitude now lost. The first two paragraphs of Letter 6 in Part III are perhaps the outstanding example.

These moments of associative recall are only one aspect of the cultivation of the past throughout the novel. 'Cet heureux temps n'est plus' is a refrain not only in moments of weakness in the second half of the story but repeatedly in the first half. There it is usually the happiness of love that is regretted, but not simply the first stage of love. Each successive stage is afterwards treated in retrospect as a lost ideal (see I, 13, 14, and 33). For Julie the ideal may be instead, or as well, the innocence of family life. 'Hélas! qu'est devenu ce temps heureux' (I, 37, p.72). 'Je tourne les yeux avec plus de regret sur l'heureux temps' (I, 63, p.120). Indeed the lovers seem almost eager to anticipate their loss. 'Hélas! j'étais heureux dans mes chimères: mon bonheur fuit avec elles', exclaims the tutor before he has even opened Julie's letter (I, 23, p.49). 'Je l'avais trop prévu', she notes in her next, 'le temps du bonheur est passé comme un éclair' (I, 25, p.52). The continual regret for past time in Rousseau's text is a kind of automatic writing, which persuades less as a function of the situations from which it nominally arises than by its own expressivity and reiteration. Alerted, we find the first example very early indeed. The tutor need wait only until his second letter to regret his first: 'avec quelle ardeur ne voudrais-je pas revenir sur le passé' (I, 2, p.12)!

Claire at the end of Part I calls the lovers 'les pauvres enfants'. Love is associated not only with innocence but with origins. When both Julie and Claire say that their own 'amitié' dates back to their infancy, we take this assertion literally. But when we are then told that the tutor has been dear to Claire 'presque dès son enfance', and he in turn claims that his ties with

Julie are 'presque dès l'enfance' (II, 18, p.182; III, 3, p.229), it is again evident that a less literal reading is required. The text deals more in myth than in mimesis. It is possible indeed to see the whole novel as a set of devices for cultivating the past. Ideologically, for example, education is to be drawn not from modern but ancient history (I, 13); the vintaging at Clarens is assimilated to the Biblical 'temps des patriarches' (V, 7). The second half of the work is the systematic revisiting of the first half, each monument and memory a cue for looking back. Revisiting in fact starts earlier: returning to Julie's bedroom the tutor recalls his earlier and happier visit (III, 14). As elsewhere, the stress on contrast serves to motivate the intensity of the evocation of the past. Retrospection as a narrative principle is also established much earlier. Re-narrating begins with the first passages of regret. Julie's first great letter on her marriage is substantially a tender retelling and re-retelling of the past. Starting with 'il ne nous sera pas pénible de rappeler un temps si cher', she goes back over the whole story. After a dozen pages of this she reprises it once more: 'rappelez-vous ces temps de bonheur et d'innocence' (III, 18). From this point onwards, guilt is also a factor to intensify awareness of the past. But has not guilt always been associated with love? 'Regret' is an ambiguous term. The novel ends with the rediscovery of the past and with a death to mourn, a new cult of the past. It is strongly suggested indeed that Saint-Preux willed the death of Julie de Wolmar in order to protect his cult of Julie d'Etange (V, 9-11; VI, 10). The past can kill. (A principle of haunting is also established: pp.107, 159, 492, 497, 567.) The novel begins with a death, that of Chaillot (I, 6). The whole text carries a title evoking the mediaeval past, and an epigraph from a long-dead poet mourning one who is gone before him. What follows, six hundred pages, is monument.

Separation in time is one kind of distancing, but there is also separation in space. The lovers are rarely together. Letter 15 of Part I sees the tutor banished from the presence of his mistress. He returns, but at the end of Part I he is sent away again. He spends the whole of Part II and most of Part III in Paris, returning just once and briefly during Julie's illness and then setting out on a tour of the world. Even before the first banishment, a brief parting prompts reflections. 'Le sort pourra bien nous séparer, mais non pas nous désunir ... nous sentirons les mêmes choses aux deux extrémités du monde' (I, 11, p.27). Physical separation can be bridged by shared feeling. Clearly there is here something similar to the bridging of temporal distance. Julie's remarks on 'le souvenir' which I quoted above began with a reference to physical absence. Later the lovers will agree that separation has compensations, even advantages. 'Quelquefois même on se voit plus souvent encore [quand on est séparés] que quand on se voyait tous les jours; car sitôt qu'un des deux est seul, à l'instant tous deux sont ensemble' (II, 15, p.167). 'Malgré l'absence, ... les puissants élancements de deux cœurs l'un vers l'autre ont toujours une volupté secrète ignorée des âmes tranquilles' (II, 16, p.173). Claire's key letter on 'fixing' time by memory also affirms the advantages of separation. Presence and memory are in fact inimical to each other — thus Wolmar's 'cure'. Presence indeed is inimical to imagination (I, 18), and to desire. Saint-Preux and Julie both reveal the object of their desire by their preference for its absence (IV, 9, p.326; IV, 13, p.374). This constitutes the evidence of love. We know that Claire loves Saint-Preux when she says 'je trouve son image plus dangereuse que sa personne', and because he says the opposite, we know that he does not love her (VI, 2, p.490; VI, 7, p.515). In the second half of the work Julie and Saint-Preux are together, but the marriage permits this, establishing and preserving the distance between them.

For the lovers, then, distance seems to be preferable. This implies on their part massive bad faith, insofar as they claim to wish to be united and they proclaim their despair at separation. Or rather, the bad faith is more on the male side. The tutor is strangely incomprehending of Julie's hints about her pregnancy, conveniently absent and ignorant for so long that the marriage to Wolmar can take place. He is always passive, allowing himself to be 'arraché', threatening only suicide. We believe more in Julie's sexual desire: she took the initiatives with the tutor; she entered the marriage. She writes to Claire and to Saint-Preux about the difficulties of continence. We believe too in the sexual desire of Claire (V, 13; VI, 2 and 6). The men however — Saint-Preux, Edouard, Wolmar — seem very skilled at forcing the women into celibacy (VI, 2, p.489; VI, 3; see *19*), but this must be because the men find female sexuality deeply disturbing (VI, 7, pp.514-15). To that extent they do indeed feel desire, repressed by or displaced as 'virtue'. The women too repeatedly link their sexuality with guilt. It is evident in turn that all this must be laid at the door of the (male) author of the novel. Bewailing the distance that it actually prefers and procures, *La Nouvelle Héloïse* is a dishonest work. In its sexual hysteria, its horror of time and change, its fear of presence, it is a very unhealthy work.

And yet surely we believe in the desire expressed most characteristically and frequently by Saint-Preux. Not a sexual desire but the desire for an absolute, for contrary absolutes: love's sweet secrets, and total transparency; the innocence of childhood and the maturity of a teacher; self-completeness and identity with the universe; sexual intensity and ideal calm; continuity and stasis; passion and virtue; nature and culture; for all the absolutes at once (no wonder the novel is 'anti-life'!). The moral and fictional forms through which this is expressed are sometimes tortured or disingenuous, but the imperative is clearly there. The figure of desire is dynamic. There is an imperative of flight. 'Il faut vous fuir, Mademoiselle' are the first words of the first letter, and this motif appears insistently throughout the first half of the novel. Yet the departure is forced: 'je ne puis vous fuir de moi-même'. To the writer himself it is incomprehensible: 'moi, vous fuir! et pourquoi?' (I, 1). The second half of the novel begins by marking the opposite movement. Its first words: 'Que tu tardes longtemps à revenir!' Return and reintegration are the principle of Clarens: 'N'ayons plus qu'une famille' (IV, 1). This ideal is almost attained: 'Le bout du monde est à votre porte'. Like the lovers in relation to each other, like the object of desire, it is so far and yet so near.

This figure of desire appears throughout the novel. 'Je touche encore au bonheur qui m'échappe' (II, 1, p.133). Happiness is close in time and space, a moment away, within reach, yet unattainable. The figure is both an image and a narrative summary, expressing with extraordinary intensity a desire which can never be fully assuaged. Julie gives this metaphorical account of her lover's relation to herself: 'Cent fois ... il s'élançait vers moi dans l'impétuosité d'un transport aveugle; il s'arrêtait tout à coup; une barrière insurmontable semblait m'avoir entourée' (I, 29, p.59). Much later, he dreams of her as she was in her youth: 'je la reconnus, quoique son visage fût couvert d'un voile. Je fais un cri, je m'élance pour écarter le voile, je ne pus l'atteindre; j'étendais les bras, je me tourmentais et ne touchais rien' (V, 9, p.466). These two images are not only parallel, but reiterated within themselves ('cent fois'; the dream is repeated; III, 13 and 14 provide another oneiric example). Often too the image may contain not just one distance but a regressive series. This pattern of *mise en abyme* (the term Gide applied to the repetition of a structure within itself) occurs in the instance that I have just quoted. Saint-Preux dreams (1), of a Julie in the past (2), whom he cannot touch (3). This is part of the episode at Villeneuve, where the 'signe mémoratif' operates, but the past time that Saint-Preux recalls with such joyous vehemence was in fact the time of his first banishment! The same is true of his experience while revisiting Meillerie. He is revisiting not Julie's past presence there but '*l'image* [qui] l'habitait jadis avec moi'. His earlier account of the episode itself already contains all these patterns. The banished tutor establishes himself on the other side of Lake Léman from Julie's dwelling. 'J'ai choisi mon asile à Meillerie sur la rive opposée; afin de jouir au moins de la vue du lieu dont je n'ose approcher.' From this distance he 'approaches' her, using in turn the naked eye, a telescope, and his imagination which retreats into the past. Each of these attempts is reiterated ('je fis mille efforts') (I, 25 and 26). Thus we have here the images of distance in parallel, each repeated in itself, the last regressive; space, time and fantasy.

How are we to understand this fundamental figure (on which, see *18*)? I take first two 'universal' interpretations. From his solitary perch at Meillerie, the tutor tells Julie, 'l'on découvre à plein la ville heureuse où vous habitez. Jugez avec quelle avidité mes yeux se portèrent vers ce séjour chéri'. This is the exile separated from the kingdom. A central myth in Western humanism tells us of a Garden of Eden, or a Golden Age, from which man is now excluded. 'L'homme est un roi dépossédé', said Pascal. The alienated protagonists of Racine and the exiles of Camus convey the same apprehension. In Rousseau the sense of a lost immediacy or plenitude is expressed in uniquely complex and rich terms (see *6*). Focused by an invented story and a poetic style, projected but highly personal, its richest expression occurs in his novel (see too *12*, *13*).

The second reading is in effect a modernist version of the Fall, expressed through psychology and linguistics. In *De la grammatologie* (1967), Jacques Derrida joins Rousseau's term 'supplément' to his own coinage 'différance'. We are constantly seeking a privileged or authentic language, which would vindicate what Derrida calls a 'metaphysics of presence'. But all expression is inadequate to our desire. We try to fill the gap of inadequacy but the supplement can only demonstrate, repeat and increase the gap. The result is an infinite deferral, of the kind reflected by Rousseau's regressive series, or an unsuccessful attempt to erase the gap, as illustrated in my paragraph in chapter 4 on the 'Elysée'. Language is a compilation of failure. Of and in his second letter the tutor writes, 'je n'écrirais point celle-ci, si je n'eusse écrit la première, et je ne veux pas redoubler ma faute, mais la réparer'. He continues to add words and add to the fault/failure/fissure.

'Deconstructionist' literary criticism is a cultural and ideological application of this analysis. It approaches texts as constructs which function — perhaps intentionally — to hide the gaps or elide the ambiguities in their own discourse. Through an insistently close rereading, often beginning with apparently minor or marginal aspects of the text, it tries to reveal the displacements and repressions operated by the writer, the culture, the language (see *22*, *23*). By definition, no final meaning can be achieved. As my accounts of happiness, distance and desire have indicated, the absolute cannot be attained, plenitude cannot be reached nor immediacy regained. Finally one may ask whether it is assumed here that Rousseau knows that this is what his text 'means'? The answer depends on — reversing or rewriting the question — what we mean by 'know', or to what extent we think that any text is not a free authorial creation but by linguistic and cultural necessity the site of contradictions. It remains true for whatever reasons that we find some texts much more complex, profound or rewarding than others. Rousseau's text itself provides ample material, often quite overtly contradicting itself (on presence and distance for example), making Rousseau his own deconstructor.

The deconstructionist bias can be put on two readings of desire that are more specific to this text. One is that so clearly set out by Claire. Distance protects the 'illusion charmante' which allows the lover to think the object of his desire perfect, thus maintaining and fixing desire. 'S'il est vrai ... que l'amour soit le plus délicieux sentiment qui puisse entrer dans le cœur humain, tout ce qui le prolonge et le fixe, même au prix de mille douleurs, est encore un bien. Si l'amour est un désir qui s'irrite par les obstacles ... il n'est pas bon qu'il soit content' (III, 7, p.235). Julie herself arrives at this view existentially, near the end. It is expressed more fully and more absolutely:

> Tant qu'on désire on peut se passer d'être heureux ... et le charme de l'illusion dure autant que la passion qui le cause. Ainsi cet état se suffit à lui-même, et l'inquiétude qu'il donne est une sorte de jouissance qui supplée à la réalité, qui vaut mieux peut-être. Malheur à qui n'a plus rien à désirer! ... L'imagination ne pare plus rien de ce qu'on possède, l'illusion cesse où commence la jouissance. Le pays des chimères est en ce monde le seul digne d'être habité, et tel est le néant des choses humaines, qu'hors l'Etre existant par lui-même, il n'y a rien de beau que ce qui n'est pas. (VI, 8, pp.527-28)

The beginning of this quotation illustrates the logic of the 'supplément'. The enjoyment of reality is supplemented by the enjoyment of an illusion, which is then declared superior. Superior because self-sufficient ... but yet involving an 'inquiétude' and therefore incomplete once more. This will lead in the letter to a new search for plenitude — 'mon âme avide cherche ailleurs de quoi se remplir' — which nothing in the human condition can satisfy. The distance cannot be closed because 'les choses humaines' always fall short of the ideal. But in any case, for the sake of maintaining the ideal, it should not be closed. It is inevitable, legitimate and wise to have recourse to 'l'illusion', 'le pays des chimères'. For Rousseau his novel itself is the ideal illusion: see my next chapter.

But the object of desire is also put at a distance because it is *forbidden*. The passage above from Julie's letter is preceded by a paragraph on her guilt. In my youth, she writes, 'je me suis mal conduite ... Pourquoi, me sentant bien-née, ai-je eu besoin de cacher ma vie?' (p.527). It is this question which leads her, through a logic of which she could not allow herself yet to be fully aware, to the discussion of desire. Only on her death-bed can the repressed object of that desire — love and the past — be uncovered. Otherwise, the forbidden must be hidden, like Julie's past life, veiled like Julie's secret heart at Clarens ('un voile de sagesse et d'honnêteté fait tant de replis autour de son cœur...', IV, 14, p.382), and like Julie in Saint-Preux's guilty dream, where the object was multiply distanced. It must be regressively hidden. Clarens hides within itself the 'Elysée' ('ce lieu ... tellement caché', IV, 11, p.353), which elides the 'bosquet' which contained the 'mystère'. The regressive series is a repressive series, offering successive substitutions so that the interdiction of the original may be obeyed — and evaded.

The 'gynécée' within Clarens, reserved for the women and children, is part of another such series. Exceptionally, Saint-Preux is admitted there, to enjoy dairy products. He lets slip a reference to the secret rendez-vous he and Julie had once planned in another dairy: '"La raison peut s'égarer dans un chalet."' Her reaction prompts his remorse (IV, 10, p.338). In this curiously awkward remark the infinitive verb is also of particular interest. Much earlier the tutor apologised for revealing 'une âme agitée qui s'égare dans ses désirs' (I, 26, p.55). Much later he will note that 'l'excès ... produit l'égarement' (VI, 7, p.521). The order of Clarens is obviously to regulate this straying, this excess. The term 'égarer' occurs in some form twice in the tutor's first letter, and twice too in that of Julie, in which they declare their guilty love. The desired is the forbidden. The interdiction — as Julie implies — intensifies the desire. 'Laisse-moi du moins connaître un égarement qui fait mon bonheur', pleads the tutor (I, 38, p.74). Rousseau's novel purports to disapprove of disordered desire, yet it constantly returns to it. Clarens failed to regulate the excess and straying of desire. Rousseau more or less wittingly fails to regulate the textual excess and straying of meaning.

6. The Prefaces and the Status of 'le roman'

Rousseau, famous for his condemnation of the decadent civilisation around him, was acutely embarrassed by his own epistolary fiction. The man who denounced the corrupting effects of contemporary culture writes a novel, a passionate love-story! The two strange Prefaces that he appends to the work are attempts to explain and justify himself. In them he criticises novels in general, while claiming that his work is different. At a time when prose fiction had a low status, novel-writers often took this line. Rousseau — predictably — goes further, presenting his work in effect as an anti-novel. But he also reveals his passionate attachment to 'le roman'. The text of *La Nouvelle Héloïse* is quite exceptionally enmeshed in that idealised literature which Rousseau has condemned. His novel itself has for him the status of a better and truer world than our own. It will be recognised as such by readers with hearts like his. This is the analysis that I shall now set out in more detail.

Rousseau uses several arguments to defend his own work which were standard among novelists in this period. 'This is not a novel', declares the Second Preface, but a 'recueil de lettres'. On the title page Rousseau in effect describes himself as the editor, the implication being that the letters are genuine. This claim (literal truth) was common among fiction writers. To criticise other novels for being full of unlikely adventures while asserting the credibility of one's own (verisimilitude) was also a commonplace. Still more so, once again as in the Second Preface, was the claim to a moral purpose (moral truth, descriptive or prescriptive). What we may note first is less what Rousseau says than the emphasis of his declarations, and their ambivalence. On the one hand, 'Jamais fille chaste n'a lu de romans'. On the other, any man who condemns me after having read the whole work could never have my respect (p.4). We may find these extreme and contradictory utterances absurd, but they reflect the intensity of Rousseau's personal engagement with fiction, as writer and as reader. 'Les romans troublent les têtes: je le crois bien. En montrant sans cesse, à ceux qui les lisent, les prétendus charmes d'un état qui n'est pas le leur, ils les séduisent ... et voilà comment on devient fou' (p.579). The attraction and the peril, which Rousseau himself knew since childhood, are as intense as that.

What particular attacks does the Second Preface make on the novel? Novels and comedies continually mock provincial life and glorify Paris (p.578). Novel language is false: 'croyez-vous que les gens vraiment passionnés aient ces manières de parler vives, fortes, coloriées que vous admirez dans vos drames et dans vos romans? Non' (p.574). Thirdly, the characters and setting are quite unreal: 'des bergers du Lignon ... [et] pareils êtres romanesques, qui ne peuvent exister que dans les livres' (p.579). Rousseau's work offers the opposite. Here is sincere language; celebration of rural life; and an ideal which his readers can see to be genuinely attainable, 'le bonheur à leur portée'. But we can show contradictions everywhere in these assertions. The most obvious is that between the first and third of Rousseau's criticisms. The novel is accused both of glorifying urbane Paris and of dealing in the pastoral fantasies of *L'Astrée*. Clearly the first is the contemporary novel, the second the old romance, but Rousseau and his culture use the same term for both, thus indicating how widely the term extends.[2] His own programme seeks to reconcile old idealism and new realism, by offering 'des hommes rares' but 'des événements communs' (p.573 paraphrased; compare the domestic sublime in Diderot).

More germane here however is the fact that he contradicts all three of his criticisms. Despite the first, Saint-Preux will declare that Parisian values and novel values are opposed. In Paris, 'les mots mêmes d'amour et d'amant sont bannis ... avec ... les romans qu'on ne lit plus'. Anyone who respected women there would be seen as 'un novice, un paladin, un homme qui n'a connu les femmes que dans les romans' (II, 21, pp.193, 198). Saint-Preux too has earlier come to reject the view that the

[2] These are the two poles of what Georges May has called *Le Dilemme du roman au XVIIIe siècle* (New Haven, Yale University Press, 1963).

language of love-novels is false. His own experience, he says, now reveals it to be authentic (I, 19, p.39). Rousseau himself in his First Preface more or less concedes this for all his protagonists by referring to 'leurs imaginations romanesques' (p.3). The dismissal of the pastoral is contradicted by his interlocutor in the Second Preface, where he identifies the main protagonists, precisely, with *L'Astrée*. 'On pr[endrait] votre petit bonhomme pour un Céladon, ... vos caillettes pour deux Astrées' (p.577). It is clear then that for every attack on the 'roman' there is also a strong identification with it. The last example shows the explicit assimilation of this allegedly unique anti-novel to preceding literature.

The very (sub)title of Rousseau's novel places it under the aegis of another collection of letters. The Héloïse-Abelard exchange was not regarded as fiction — but its numerous recent treatments had certainly placed it in the literary domain. In the Second Preface he calls his novel 'une longue romance' (p.577). Once more Saint-Preux picks this up within the fiction, explaining the qualities of what we might call the 'ballad' and stating that its language of love is that which he and Julie had used as lovers (V, 7, p.461). In fact, the language to which the couple and Claire more readily have recourse is that of Italian poetry. Lines, couplets and quatrains of lyric and dramatic verse, principally from Petrarch, Tasso and the contemporary Metastasio, repeatedly provide the trio with their expression. They provide indeed an intertext for the novel. And of course the same source provides its epigraph, two lines from Petrarch. Then there are the frequent invocations of classical culture, allusions to Plutarch being the most common. (Plutarch and *L'Astrée* were the two ideal book-worlds of Rousseau's childhood, he tells us in his autobiographical works.) The identification with the Graeco-Roman is reiterated. At Clarens things are named for Apollo, Lucullus, Elysium. In the first half the lovers clutch at such references. The tutor cannot threaten suicide without calling on Sappho, or Julie offer a rendez-vous without citing the temple of Cnidus. Throughout, Rousseau's novel insistently assimilates itself to a great domain: literary culture, usually in its high forms and almost always from the past.

Essentially this is the domain of the 'romanesque'. It provides the characters and Rousseau himself with an identification and an ideal. The Second Preface also offers other identifications which give the 'roman' clearer ideological and even ontological weight. *La Nouvelle Héloïse*, says Rousseau, shows us 'un petit monde différent du nôtre'. This seems remarkably similar to what he says about love, which he calls 'un autre univers'. More fully, 'l'amour n'est qu'illusion; il se fait pour ainsi dire un autre univers'. Then he calls this 'le souvenir' (pp.574-75). Julie's pen-ultimate letter will provide a third text on 'the other world'. 'Le pays des chimères est en ce monde le seul digne d'être habité.' It is clear then that 'roman', 'amour', 'souvenir' and 'chimère' are ultimately interchangeable in Rousseau's metalanguage. It is evident too that he has quite lost sight of his social programme. Only the middle part of the Second Preface is concerned with the public mission of his novel. The beginning and end are pre-occupied with it as a personal experience for writer and reader, in which the question of its moral status is inseparable from that of its ontological status. Is this other world true? For the inhabitants of our own corrupted world, of course not. 'La correspondance entière est-elle une fiction? Gens du monde, que vous importe? C'est sûrement une fiction pour vous' (p.3). Evasive but aggressive, Rousseau is saying that the world of the 'roman' is more real, more true, than the degenerate historical world we live in daily. It constitutes the condemnation of our world, offering consolation and answering our deepest needs. Or does it simply express them? Is it only an illusion, a chimera? (Note how often Rousseau's correspondents are made to report their key moments of revelation with a preliminary 'je crus ...', 'il me sembla ...') This world *is* not, but perhaps it *was* (p.585), like love or like the past surviving only in memory, like the state of nature in the *Discours sur l'inégalité*. Can we say that it is unreal but authentic? But it is also profoundly dangerous. It is the world of desire, which Rousseau knows to be forbidden. It disturbs order in the present, order in the world, order in the mind. It seduces. This is his guilt at his own writing. Thus he identifies with it and repudiates it, moves closer and moves away. He treats it as independent, yet he maintains the umbilical link so as to claim the glory and the guilt. 'Je me nomme ... à la tête de ce recueil, non pour me l'approprier, mais pour en répondre' (p.3).

Perhaps we can now define how Rousseau wishes to see his own role in relation to the 'roman' he gives us. He calls himself its editor. The hoary old pretence is in fact the key. The ideal world does exist, whether within his mind and memory, or in some external reality, independently of him. (Thus too the Platonic 'divin modèle'.) He *transcribes* it. In the Second Preface we find several times the notion of a truthful transcription. To produce a work like this is to '*tenir registre* de ce que chacun peut voir tous les jours' (p.573). Each missive has the quality of 'une lettre que l'amour a *réellement dictée*' (p.574). The latter is a statement about writers within the work. There too we find transcription which is faithful, simple, *unmediated*. Each lover claims to write authentically, to transcribe his or her own truth. When Julie retells her story, she calls this 'le *fidèle* tableau, la *naïve* histoire de ma vie' (III, 18, p.364). To the 'histoire' and writing we must add the 'tableau' and showing. The Second Preface promises '*un spectacle* véritablement nouveau' (p.575). For we are dealing with a vision. Is not the 'illumination de Vincennes' still the model? 'Oh monsieur, si j'avais pu *écrire* le quart de ce que j'ai *vu* ..., j'aurai fait *voir*' (*Lettres à Malesherbes*, ii). Rousseau collects up, transcribes, edits the letters. Faithfully he shows forth this better world.

Within this harmonious novel, all the correspondents are members of the one fortunate group. They have a similar perspective. The writer of a letter knows that the recipient will recognise his authenticity and understand him, because they share the truth and the ideal. This is what Rousseau looks for in us, his readers. If we are worthy, his heart will speak directly to ours, because we share the vision. I hope that I have at least shown how profound and rich I find this vision. My last two chapters look at Rousseau's aesthetic achievement within the epistolary form, and at the historical significance of his new model of relations between author, literary work and reader.

7. An Epistolary Novel:
Form and Aesthetic Achievement

From seventeenth-century to eighteenth-century prose fiction, a most important development is the shift from third-person to first-person narration. Characteristically, the ominscient narrator of the previous century is replaced by 'I'. Thus the narrator becomes identified with the protagonist, and the experience recounted becomes more immediate in turn for the reader. Most of the novels that we now admire incorporate this new subjectivity. Its principal forms are the memoir-novel, and then — with as many narrators as there are letter-writers — the epistolary novel.

By genre, thus, Rousseau's novel is of its time. Perhaps Richardson's *Clarissa*, and the much imitated model of Héloïse's letters to Abelard, were particular influences on his own choice of the letter form. Here though we can already begin to see what distinguishes his work. It has the amplitude and the multiple voices of Richardson, but it combines this with French thematic concentration, aesthetic idealisation and unity of tone. Comparison with the final epistolary masterpiece of the century is even more revealing. In *Les Liaisons dangereuses* the letter form is structurally and thematically organic. If Rousseau's novel is indeed about distance and desire, the generic choice is also deeply appropriate. As one critic has observed, 'The letters assume and in fact establish separation and then proceed to abolish it' (*9*, p.72). To write a letter is to try to bridge a gap, perhaps to evade an interdiction, to unite oneself by writing and in sentiment with that which is apart. Between the lovers indeed the letters do not just narrate events, or interpret them. To some extent they *are* the events. The relationship begins by letter. It is nurtured, cancelled, finally renewed, and announced triumphant, by letter. The passionate personal involvement so characteristic of Rousseau himself as a writer lends itself well to an epistolary novel of love. On the other hand, his anxiety to declare his own positions causes problems. The didactic 'digressions' are often ill-placed; the characters must also assume responsibility for the admiring compliments that Rousseau wishes to pay them; and even then he cannot resist appending numerous footnotes — mostly irritable — as 'Editor'.

From the point of view of verisimilitude there are weaknesses in his use of the letter-form. We can believe that the tutor might have had recourse to a letter for his initial declaration of love. Once Julie has replied, it seems unlikely that they would continue to write while seeing each other every day. The most absurd letter is the notorious missive penned by the tutor outside Julie's bed chamber as she arrives (I, 54). Such distancings and deferrals, as I have indicated, have deeper reasons. Some of Claire's letters to her neighbour Julie also seem unlikely. They reflect not circumstantial necessity but Rousseau's need for a narrator. Verbatim recall of a conversation (I, 48 or 62) is perhaps no less unsatisfactory a convention than in any first-person narrative. Some of the didactic digressions in Part I are awkwardly placed (I, 35 on jealousy; I, 57, on the duel). The long set-pieces later, on the other hand, seem appropriate to the philosophical bias and slow pace of Clarens. Clearly Edouard must be absent from Clarens so that Saint-Preux has someone to write all these pieces to. But it seems to me that the former's other functions in the fiction make his role here entirely appropriate. In general Rousseau handles his multiple correspondents with great skill and classical formal balance. All his five major characters both send and receive letters.[3] Astonishingly, the numbers sent and received are approximately equal in every case (from the tutor's 65/62 to Wolmar's 6/4). This balance applies even to Fanchon, d'Orbe and the Baron d'Etange. The rare exceptions seem to have their logic. Only Julie's mother receives a letter (III, 2) without sending one — she would scarcely have had the strength, poor thing. Only Claire's daughter Henriette sends one (V, 14) without receiving one — as Julie notes in IV, 1, children are unsatisfactory interlocutors.

---

[3] For the various statistics that follow, and some of the conclusions drawn from them, I am indebted to *8*.

In relation to thematic structure, a study of the patterning of letters over the whole work is most rewarding. The novel is divided into six Parts, the letters numbered separately in each Part. It is a remarkable fact that each successive Part contains a decreasing number of letters. This itself constitutes a structural pattern, suggesting a movement towards stasis. Such organic progression (or regression) is also reflected in other ways. I, 1-5 is a series of short letters; VI, 11, the antepenultimate letter, is the longest in the work. (Between these extremes, III, 18, is longer than any letter preceding it, but is itself exceeded by IV, 10, and V, 2 and 3). Marking narrative structure, the relative number of letters between Julie and the tutor reflects closely the fortunes of their relationship. Part I consists almost entirely of the lovers' letters to each other. The first decisive separation sees a greater role for other correspondents (the first half of Part II), then the couple regain domination of the exchanges. In Part III their liaison is never dominant numerically or morally. Julie's marriage literally determines the demise of their correspondence. She brings it back to life in VI, 6, where her love for Saint-Preux may be read between the lines. This permits the final revelation of VI, 12 to be addressed to him.

Closely linked to theme, the headings Rousseau gives to the letters are very significant.[4] Every letter between the couple in Parts I-III is headed either 'De Julie' or 'A Julie', or simply 'Réponse'. (In their resumed correspondence of VI, 6 and 8 she is designated 'Mme de Wolmar', as she has been in headings generally since IV, 1. But in VI, 12, pointedly, she is once more 'Julie'.) The principle implicit here in fact applies in all the letters where she is sender or receiver. She is constantly named in the headings, making her in effect the centre to which things come and whence they flow. The tutor on the other hand, even under his pseudonym, is never designated in the headings. Perhaps this suggests that he is Everyman. Or the outsider. Or the implicit narrator, if not also author, of the whole: the absence betraying Rousseau's presence? 'I' needs no other

---

[4] N.B. the Garnier-Flammarion edition fails to indicate that the 'Table des matières' included at the end, which names a sender and a receiver for each letter, is *not by Rousseau*. Its textual status is doubtful (see *1*, pp.lxxiii and 1825). I refer exclusively to the heading that precedes each letter.

name.

Rousseau's aesthetic achievement in his novel is quite exceptional. The observations of one critic have brought out very well its symphonic quality (*1*). His style is highly musical. Unique however are the rhythm and tone, the contrasts and harmony, that he imparts to this long work through the letter form itself. I look first at variety and contrast.

The epistolary mode of narration must tend to discontinuity, when more than one writer is involved. Breaks in time will be reinforced by changes in style and point of view. Variety of tone is notable here at the beginning of letters. The openings of some are desperately urgent: 'Tout est perdu! Tout est découvert!' Others stern: 'Je n'ai point voulu vous expliquer hier'. Some roguish: 'Ah mauvaise!' Some bitter: 'Tenez, cruelle, voilà ma réponse'. Some are grave: 'Je me suis attendu, cher Bomston, au dénouement de vos longues aventures'. Some elegiac: 'Enfin le voile est déchiré; cette longue illusion est évanouie'. Most of the dramatic openings, like the dramatic events, occur in the first three Parts. Here Rousseau uses effects of contrast. The voluptuous bubble is pricked by harsh reality (I, 15 then 16; or I, 55 then 56), marking the theme of the 'court bonheur'. He shows admirable handling of groups of letters, in relation to the story and for a kind of organic rhythm. Consider the opening of the novel. I, 1-5, form a first group. Within it, the tutor's declaration becomes progressively more urgent in three letters which are successively shorter, leading to a climax of five rapid 'billets': a veritable stichomythia. The exchange then opens out into Julie's full reply, and the movement is completed and closed by the tutor, in two letters of contrasting tone and equal length. Then I, 6 and 7 form a group and provide a new dimension. Letters 8 and after return to the dialogue of the couple two months on. The first significantly longer letters (I, 12 on education; I, 23 on the Valais) also widen our perspective. On a larger scale, Part II falls into an emotionally disordered first half of shorter letters (1-10), contrasted by the serenity of the second dominated by the long accounts of Paris. The latter section in turn is suddenly interrupted by the dramatic revelation of the last letter. Part II indeed is a kind of *mise en abyme* of the whole, with Paris as the anti-utopia foreshadowing Clarens, and the discovered passion at the end of each linked with death and decisive separation/remembrance. All the particular structures are overarched by the pattern of the whole.

The rhythm of passion is rapid, an effect conveyed by the multiple shorter letters of Parts I-III. That of Clarens is slow and deliberate as in the long accounts of IV and V. The dénouement also repeats another important device that Rousseau has used earlier, the multiplying of letters around a single subject. At its most abstract, it may resemble the 'philosophical' principle of plural views on some general issue (the opposed letters on suicide: III, 21-22). More organic are the successive commentaries of Claire, the tutor and Julie herself upon the couple's sexual union (I, 29-31). Or the successive reactions of Saint-Preux, Claire and Wolmar to the young man's dream (V, 9-11). This dream in turn recalls for us 'l'inoculation de l'amour', first in Julie's delirious vision then in Claire's account (III, 15-16). Again we become aware both of internal echoes and of formal doublings and triplings within the text — of which the overall repetition of the itinerary is the fullest realisation. Basic too is a particular form of doubling, by which a very short 'news-bulletin' letter precedes a long reflective account of the same event. Its most elaborate occurrence is near the end. Fanchon, then Claire, briefly apprise us of Julie's accident and then her death, clearing the way for the full inter-pretative exploration by Wolmar that follows. But there are simpler versions. Claire announces Julie's marriage in a note of one paragraph, so that Julie can give its narrative and meaning thirty pages (III, 17-18). Julie informs us in five lines that she has surmounted the peril of the 'promenade sur le lac', thus leaving us free to undergo the moral and affective process itself in the subsequent long letter by Saint-Preux (IV, 16-17).

This device produces a complementarity of content, and one of form. The effect of both is to *slow down*. The narrative halts or repeats itself so that we may draw from it the fullest experience. Time stops or repeats itself so that we may live the miracle of continuity instead of continual change. (Once again the over-arching structure is Parts IV-VI covering again Parts

I-III.) We should notice Rousseau's penchant for tableaux. 'Dieux! quel ravissant *spectacle*' exclaims the tutor (I, 38, p.73); Clarens is 'un *tableau* si ravissant' (IV, 10, p.352). There are over a score of similar uses in the text. The painterly term implies a static art — ideally the 'immobilité d'extase' of V, 3. The term from the theatre suggests a certain stylisation and distancing, collective ritual movement contemplated. These tableaux occur within letters which themselves sometimes depict rather than tell. The outstanding example of course is the 'Vendanges' letter, in which both our terms occur (p.457). That letter is narrated in the present tense. Is this the dramatic present and 'writing to the moment' (the devices used respectively in the middle and at the end of Fanchon's letter VI, 9)? Or is it the timeless present (as in IV, 10 or V, 2)? The instant and eternity ...

The Second Preface appears to affirm that there is little difference between the epistolary style of the various protagonists. It is observed that 'dans une société très intime, les styles se rapprochent ainsi que les caractères', here a happy phenomenon for which Julie is given special credit (p.585). This principle is clearly fundamental to the 'harmony' of the novel, indicating the relative unimportance of the story, even of the external life in general. Letters tell, describe or analyse, or express intense feeling. But they all do so in a moral and sentimental perspective (at its worst, remorseless moralising) which constitutes the reason for writing. The writer moreover almost always addresses someone whom he knows will share his perspective. This is not to say that there are no differences. All the main protagonists differ in their characteristics, and it has been persuasively shown that each person is indeed differentiated by his or her manner of writing (7, pp.139-53). But there are no genuine oppositions, only complementarities. Their feelings, and their language, approach unison. Thus the epistolary mode, which one would expect to be necessarily discontinuous in time and in point of view, becomes here a kind of harmony. To this the convention governing the headings of the letters makes another notably simple contribution. Very few, as I remarked earlier, give the names of both the writer and the addressee. None is dated.

These mere externals — individuals, calendar time — are thus deprecated. To 'situate' the letter we must read it, plunge into it. There we will find shared feeling and lived time.

8. An Eighteenth-century Novel and Beyond: Historical Significance

La Nouvelle Héloïse is in some ways a typical mid-eighteenth century French novel. Most of its protagonists are of the nobility (the English novel has long been more bourgeois). The plot centres upon love, frustrated by social prejudice. Artistic, social and philosophical issues are debated. Paris is depicted and satirised by an 'outsider'; an ideal alternative is sketched in. Nature and feeling are celebrated, and especially the 'volupté' of 'vertu'. The mode is discursive, sentimental and didactic. Rousseau uses the fashionable epistolary form (see my previous chapter). He resorts to traditional romance *topoi* (the portrait of the beloved, the voyage of the rejected lover), and narrative devices (the dramatic beginning *in medias res*; reversals and mystifications). His style is elevated, his diction mainly abstract. He attempts to ally this classical rhetoric with the new concern for immediacy. Thus we have the first-person narration, the concern for morally-didactic impact, and the pursuit of the domestic sublime. Occasionally we encounter 'writing to the moment', or the 'style entrecoupé' (as in I, 28). At its worst this amalgam produces pompous, ideologically-weighted cliché. Mme d'Etange is always 'la plus tendre des mères'; the tutor is not simply 'tired' but 'vaincu par la nature'. But here we are already slipping into the new, so let us turn to it.

Rousseau's protagonists and setting are marginal to francophone culture. The families of Julie and Claire are petty rural nobility, as well as Swiss. Within the cultural conventions of the time this makes them doubly subjects for ridicule. They are not so clearly outside French norms as to make them exotic (Edouard and Wolmar are more difficult cases). Nor are they sketched lightly, vehicles for some broader authorial purpose. They are firmly located in a specific and unfashionable rural milieu. The local names are named — Vevey, Clarens, Meillerie ... We are given something of the local topography (the lake, the mountains) and mores (the Fanchon episode, the Valais). The situation and life are domestic. There is a certain amount of concrete reference (walking, fishing, harvesting), and vocabulary (Julie's clothing, the flora of the 'Elysée', the 'matinée à l'anglaise'). The letter-writers include a peasant-girl and a child. There is allusion to the heroine's miscarriage — vulgar if not scandalous in literary terms. Undignified details occasionally appear elsewhere, notably in the unremitting account of Julie's death. In fact, quantitatively there is relatively little exterior 'realism' in the novel, but we are kept aware of the everyday dimension, which is very important. It is one of the three literary elements that Rousseau uniquely combines, the others being the epistolary form and the language of extreme states. The subjective sensibilities of his correspondents must constantly hold together this mundane situation and their interior life of absolute aspiration.

In a sense, though, the whole work is an interior life, in a new transcription. Rousseau has written a long novel, but one which moves very slowly. There are few 'events'. There are no villains. There is little conflict (except that endemic to the condition of being human). But there is much complementarity, of which the virtuous 'ménage à trois' at Clarens is the most remarkable example. In an age when to cause boredom and to arouse ridicule were the two worst crimes in civilised society, Rousseau risks both. He throws into its teeth his ideal fiction, challenging his urbane readers to believe in it or to reveal by their disbelief their own corruption. In an age where we find no real poetry, he writes a poetic novel. Poetic in the sense of visionary; in that of lyric, conveying intense emotional states; and in the sense of being aesthetically structured by image and sound and rhythm. His language is not entirely decorous and correct, because it also seeks to be harmonious and expressive. He was quite conscious of the distinction (see his Note to VI, 8, p.528). His vocabulary is 'poetic' in the traditional sense of being elevated, but also in that it tries to seize and convey sensations. As befits the man who subscribed to 'le matérialisme du sage', he shows that the moral is close to the physical. The key terms in his moral vocabulary are intensely sensual: 'souffrir', 'languir', 'guérir', 'jouir', 'volupté', 'extase'. His language tries to reproduce the experience, or even to become the experience. The whole has its own continuity. 'Couler' is a verb which Rousseau uses admirably. In his novel time flows, feeling flows, writing flows. 'Une lettre d'un amant, ... son cœur plein d'un sentiment qui déborde, [est] comme une source vive qui coule sans cesse et ne s'épuise jamais' (p.574). Time and feeling then are almost co-extensive with writing. This novel approaches the modern condition of being about itself. Mimetic elements are resumed into a vast system of internal correspondences and harmonies.

Onomastics — the study of proper names — is an aspect that I have had to leave aside. It serves to illustrate the interior harmony, and to lead us out again to exterior meaning. Commonplace names here are transfigured by their context to take on both literal and symbolic significance. 'Claire' and 'Clarens' connote clarity, thus transparency, purity. 'Etang(e)' links Julie with the lake, thus with love and death ('un "lac d'amour" où l'on se noie' in the ambiguous Genevan pronunciation: VI, 5, p.502). She is drawn to the lake as the tutor is drawn to the mountains, an elemental decor at once in harmony with their simple lives and secretly hostile to the civil order they have entered.

These great natural phenomena are still heavily 'moralised', and they occupy as narrative elements only a modest place in Rousseau's novel. They constitute nevertheless a presence both symbolic and sensual which marks a new 'sentiment de la nature'. The elemental forces are the preferred alternative to Paris, to Vevey, even ultimately to Clarens, offering a truth and a communion which the alienated individual cannot find in society. Here is a second great Romantic theme anticipated by Rousseau. A third of course is that of time, loss and memory: 'O temps, suspends ton vol'. A fourth the cult of the ideal, and of death. All imply the aspiration to the absolute, the refusal of social and indeed worldly limits, which is so foreign to the classical and humanist wisdom of the previous age.

La Nouvelle Héloïse was an immediate and enormous success with the reading public. By the time of the Revolution it had gone through some seventy editions. This is remarkable enough.

What was unique however was the response that it aroused. 'The reception accorded to it demonstrated for the first time the power of a novel to affect its readers emotionally and transform their view of life' (*26*, p.227). We know this because literally dozens of people were moved to write to its author, most to say that his book spoke for them. They responded especially to the characters and their feelings, though some were uneasy about the morality of the first half. They identified mainly with what one might call the bourgeois-sentimental dimension, the cult of the family and of virtue. To that extent they vindicate the moral and social programme that Rousseau claims for his novel in the Second Preface (pp.577-81).

Proto-Romantic alienation, and bourgeois familial virtues, seem difficult to reconcile (though they cohabit in *La Nouvelle Héloïse* itself, and then in the nineteenth century). The link here perhaps is in the relation between the individual and fictional writing. Each of these acquires greater importance, as does the relation between them, to the detriment of social norms. For Rousseau and his enthused reader alike, the world he has created is more satisfying, and more real, than that around them. They identify with it, intensely and openly. And many of his readers identified Rousseau himself with his work, in a way no one would have dreamed of with Racine or Prévost or Voltaire. They thought it was his own story. Here there are biographical factors (the Swiss connection; his only novel), and literary factors (the epistolary pretence; the hiding of the tutor's real name). He himself did nothing to discourage the error. In fact we know that in an important sense this was indeed a confessional novel. The *Confessions* tell us that it was born of personal fantasy, and that he based the tutor on himself. What he reveals about himself in his autobiographical works makes evident not only the use and transformation of incidents in his own life (the Parisian brothel; the return), but also the narcissism, the therapeutic value, and the strong presence of private myths in his fiction. We know this from works which were written after his novel; his early readers were the more perspicacious in seeing the link beforehand. But the point is equally that Rousseau then wants to *tell* us. He insists on the personal sources of his art. His novel is not just

one more social artefact, but the expression of the intimate life
of its creator. In the Prefaces he identifies himself passionately
with his creation and his characters. In his fictional writing there
is none of the ironic distance we associate with the age of wit.
Certainly there is aesthetic distance, for he is a conscious as well
as a consummate craftsman, but at times it is lost in the intensity
of his moral and emotional engagement with his fiction. With
Rousseau the literary product becomes an icon, a challenge to
and substitute for society. The writing and reading of literature
are becoming acts of private communion or self-communion.
Society will duly re-incorporate its own productions. This is the
beginning of what Paul Bénichou has called 'le sacre de
l'écrivain'.

Select Bibliography

I have tried to provide a conspectus. Items are grouped by theme or approach. Where the scope of an item is not clear from its title, I have given a summary indication.

The most authoritative editions of *La Nouvelle Héloïse*, with substantial introductions and notes, are those by

1. Bernard Guyon, in vol. 2 (1964) of the *Œuvres complètes* (Paris, Gallimard, Bibliothèque de la Pléiade, 4 vols, 1959-69). Particularly good on internal criticism and aesthetic qualities.
2. Daniel Mornet, 4 vols (Paris, Hachette, Les Grands Ecrivains de la France, 1925). Particularly good on literary and intellectual history.

GOOD SHORT GENERAL STUDIES

3. Henri Coulet, *Le Roman jusqu'à la Révolution* (Paris, Colin, 1975), pp.401-17, '*La NH*'.
4. Jean Rousset, 'Rousseau romancier: *La NH*', in *Jean-Jacques Rousseau*, ed. Samuel Baud-Bovy *et al.* (Neuchâtel, La Baconnière, 1962), pp.67-80.
5. Lionel Gossman, 'The worlds of *La NH*', *Studies on Voltaire and the Eighteenth Century* (hereinafter *SVEC*), 41 (1966), pp.235-76.
6. Jean Starobinski, *Jean-Jacques Rousseau: la transparence et l'obstacle* (Paris, Plon, 1957; augmented edition, Paris, Gallimard, 1971), ch. 5, '*La NH*'.
7. J.-L. Lecercle, *Rousseau et l'art du roman* (Paris, Colin, 1969), Part II, '*Julie*'.

STRUCTURE

8. Patrick Brady, 'Structural affiliations of *La NH*', *L'Esprit Créateur*, 9 (1969), pp.207-20.
9. Hugh M. Davidson, 'Dialectical order and movement in *La NH*' in *Enlightenment Studies in Honour of Lester D. Crocker* (Oxford, The Voltaire Foundation, 1979), pp.71-86.

PHILOSOPHICAL

10. Etienne Gilson, *Les Idées et les lettres* (Paris, Vrin, 1932; new ed. 1955), pp.275-98, 'La méthode de M. de Wolmar'.
11. Madeleine B. Ellis, '*La NH*: a synthesis of Rousseau's thought* (Toronto, University of Toronto Press, 1949).

12. Christie McDonald Vance, *The Extravagant Shepherd: a study of the pastoral vision in 'La NH'*, *SVEC*, 105 (1973).

13. James F. Jones, *'La NH': Rousseau and utopia* (Geneva, Droz, 1978).

14. Robert Mauzi, 'Le problème religieux dans *La NH*' in Fabre, J., *et al.* (eds), *Jean-Jacques Rousseau et son œuvre* (Paris, Klincksieck, 1964), pp.159-70.

15. J.-L. Bellenot, 'Les formes de l'amour dans *La NH*', *Annales de la Société Jean-Jacques Rousseau* (hereinafter *AJJR*), 33 (1953-55), pp.149-207.

16. Bernard Guyon, 'La mémoire et l'oubli dans *La NH*', *AJJR*, 35 (1959-62), pp.49-71.

17. François Van Laere, *Une Lecture du temps dans 'La NH'* (Neuchâtel, La Baconnière, 1968).

18. R.J. Howells, 'Désir et distance dans *La NH*', *SVEC*, 230 (1985), pp.223-32.

19. Anne de Fabry, *Essais autour de 'La NH'* (Sherbrooke, Naaman, 1977). The 'ascension' of Saint-Preux and of Jean-Jacques.

20. David L. Anderson, 'Edouard and Jean-Jacques in retrospect', *L'Esprit Créateur*, 9 (1969), pp.219-26. Uses 'Les amours de milord Edouard Bomston'.

21. M.-H. Huet, *Le Héros et son double* (Paris, Corti, 1975), ch. 4, '*La NH*'. Saint-Preux and society.

22. Tony Tanner, *Adultery in the Novel* (Baltimore, Johns Hopkins University Press, 1979), ch. 2, 'Rousseau's *La NH*'. Approach is deconstructionist, Freudian.

23. Peggy Kamuf, *Fictions of Feminine Desire* (Lincoln, University of Nebraska Press, 1982), ch. 4, '*Julie, or the New Héloïse*'. Deconstructionist. Feminist.

LITERARY ANTECEDENTS, RECEPTION (on influence see *2*, vol. 1)

24. Henri Coulet, '*La NH* et la tradition romanesque française', *AJJR*, 37 (1966-68), pp.35-55.

25. Laurent Versini, *Laclos et la tradition* (Paris, Klincksieck, 1968), Part II, ch. 2, 'La tradition épistolaire'.

26. Anna Attridge, 'The reception of *La NH*', *SVEC*, 120 (1974), pp.227-67.

CRITICAL GUIDES TO FRENCH TEXTS

edited by

Roger Little, Wolfgang van Emden, David Williams